BOOK 2

STUDIOS. SALESMEN. SHRINES. SURFSPOTS.

PAPERBACK L.A.

A CASUAL ANTHOLOGY

EDITOR
SUSAN LaTEMPA

PROSPECT
·PARK·
BOOKS

Published by Prospect Park Books
2359 Lincoln Ave.
Altadena, CA 91001
www.prospectparkbooks.com

Distributed by Consortium
www.cbsd.com

Library of Congress Cataloging in Publication Data is on file with the Library of Congress. The following is for reference only:

Names: LaTempa, Susan
Titles: Paperback L.A. Book 2: Studios. Salesmen. Shrines. Surfspots. (2018)
Identifiers: ISBN 978-1-945551-37-6 (flexibound)
Subjects: Los Angeles, Calif.; anthologies; essays; photography.

Design by Michelle Ingram (with Kathy Kikkert)
Cover photo: *River Blues*, under Olympic Blvd. bridge, Los Angeles, 2010, by Danny Martinez

Printed in Korea

And it's not my fault that this town shakes
I saw the falling rocks and I hit my brakes
I've come a long way, I've gone 500 miles today
I've come a long way, you can travel for miles
And never leave L.A.

"COME A LONG WAY"
MICHELLE SHOCKED
1992

CONTENTS

PAPERBACK L.A. BOOK 2 IS A CASUAL ANTHOLOGY.

A casual anthology deserves a casual intro. Let's begin with a few FAQs.

Do I need to read *Paperback L.A. Book 1, A Casual Anthology: Clothes. Coffee. Crushes. Crimes.* to enjoy *Paperback L.A. Book 2, A Casual Anthology: Studios. Salesmen. Shrines. Surfspots.?*

No. Each book in this series is a stand-alone with its own personality.

Does this book cover a certain time period?

No. Each selection takes place in a different era. The written pieces are arranged in chronological order of the events described.

What kinds of stories are in here?

Excerpts from novels. Short stories, histories, memoirs, a recipe. Magazine and newspaper articles and excerpts. A television broadcast transcript. A timeline and an essay written especially for this book.

Do the photo essays go with certain stories?

No. They go in between.

What's the idea behind the *Paperback L.A.* series?

The idea is to keep refreshing the guest list at the patio party so the conversation about L.A. stays lively and thought-provoking.

There. That takes care of the preliminaries.

The selections I've gathered made their way into this book via as many routes as people make their way to L.A. Some had been on my bookshelves for years, waiting to be more widely shared. Some were born with this book. Others landed in *Paperback L.A. Book 2* through research, referral, recommendation, and rumor.

I had read Diana Serra Cary's book *Hollywood's Children: An Inside Account of the Child Star Era* when it was published, and it stayed in my personal library as a pivotal work on Hollywood. For the *Paperback L.A.* series, I wanted from the start to anchor this second volume with selections from it. Born in 1918, Cary went to work in a Hollywood studio before she was two years old as Baby Peggy, a national sensation in the silent era. Her take on Los Angeles is unique. "I could find hundreds of studies about the effects of children watching too many movies," she told a *Guardian* reporter in 2015 about her reasons for writing *Hollywood's Children,* "but nothing about the effects of being in them."

Other substantial reads are excerpts from fiction by Gina B. Nahai and Jim

Gavin. Nahai has said that her novel *Moonlight on the Avenue of Faith* is based on stories told by several different people, and her Los Angeles has vividly specific local geographies. She crafts a newcomer-to-L.A. story like no other. Gavin, too, brings impressive abilities to his form—in this case, the short story. In selecting "Costello" for this book from his collection of short stories, *Middle Men,* I was, it turns out, joining a wide group of admirers. Although I wasn't surprised to find that the seemingly modest story of a plumbing-parts salesman debuted in *The New Yorker*, it still feels like my very own discovery. I know this character's territory, from OC backyards to public golf courses, and I was glad to spend time with him. As my publisher says of this story, "It got to me."

Chester Himes is known for his 1945 novel *If He Hollers Let Him Go,* an L.A. classic, written when the author had battled segregation in the fast-expanding wartime industries. The story included here, "Lunching at the Ritzmore," was published a few years earlier and is a richly descriptive joke about the absurdity of L.A.'s hypocritical status quo.

Three selections in this volume are tagged as ghost towns, a term usually applied to places like mining towns or ruins of half-built developments—empty places built on past dreams. I've applied the label to stories of communities lost through extermination, internment, or gentrification.

Benjamin Madley's evocation of California before contact with Europeans names scores of communities and their agricultural, hunting, cultural, and other practices. It's a litany that refutes centuries of dismissive accounts of indigenous Californians as lacking "real" villages, religions, or leaders. Naomi Hirahara's essay about one mystery of Terminal Island stands in for all the stories interrupted and lost when Japanese immigrants and Japanese Americans were forcibly relocated and their homes bulldozed after Pearl Harbor. As a ghost town, Fish Harbor has virtually no visual remains, but it exists nevertheless because of the actions of former residents to preserve their place-based identities and to document and remember.

And famous sci-fi writer Ray Bradbury's spooky descriptions of Venice recall the day when it was a cheap, run-down seaside neighborhood with amusement park ruins and decaying "Italian" villas and arcades, now a ghost town hidden under layers of subsequent real estate development.

INTRODUCTION
SUSAN
LaTEMPA

Racing through the decades, "Hot, Fast, and Dangerous," a timeline by Preston Lerner, organizes a century of significant dates into one fast-moving narrative. Covering the century when L.A. was a motor-sports mecca, Lerner pinpoints the rise and fall of racetracks, the nation's first speed shop, the births of hot rodding, drag racing, kustom cars, and more.

To call attention to our metro outdoors, three "Nature Notes" are dispersed in this book. Nature Note 1 is a stranger-than-fiction agriculture story about mustard-harvesting machines in the nineteenth century. For Nature Note 2, Hartmut Walter's breathtaking portfolio "Wild Birds in L.A." draws from his archive of more than 20,000 bird photos. Nature Note 3 is a snapshot of a midcentury avocado moment.

Danny Martinez's photo subjects range from the Hollywood sign as seen from Boyle Heights, offering a matter-of-fact sense of scale and distance, to a Quinceañera group between poses, comfortably inhabiting an iconic adult corridor of power. Another subculture takes the stage in the portraits in Ann Summa's warm and appealing portrayals of bike riders who show how embedded "outdoor activity" is in the city's days—and nights.

Family stories are often imbued with a sense of place, and at *Westways,* I edited two family memoirs that stayed with me so completely I could paraphrase them years later. I selected them to reprint here: Colleen Dunn Bates's wry account of her father's cool period, and Eric Gutierrez's perfectly pitched ode to a young family in a young era.

Finally, a newspaper editor once told me of seeing a man buy the paper at a newsstand and then pull out the sports section, tossing the rest in a trash can. Yes, some of us buy a publication mostly for whatever divertissement we're addicted to, so this anthology is also anchored by stellar shorts: a pair of Wendy Gilmartin's hilariously accurate fugly building columns from *LA Weekly*, and a gem of an account of early social life in the pueblo from merchant José Arnaz.

SUSAN LaTEMPA
LOS ANGELES, 2018

P.S. Please see the acknowledgments page for important thanks due to our contributors. Special thanks for *Book 2* are extended to Matt Kresling for the *Paperback L.A.* video trailer, to Arianna DeSano for tech support, to Hal Barron for book lists, and to Michelle Ingram DeLong and Leilah Bernstein for joining the team.

In *An American Genocide* (2016), historian Benjamin Madley presents a detailed month-by-month narrative as well as 200 pages of appendixes to document his finding that the extermination of California Indians was genocide. The numbers, numbers, numbers are chilling. The role of government is exposed. And making it possible were rights-restricting laws under Spanish, Mexican, and American rule, some of which were still on the books in the 1930s. Spain classified indigenous adults as minors, allowing the enslavement of mission laborers. Mexican rule transferred a peonage system to the ranchos. In 1850, the new state of California eliminated Indians' right to vote or testify in court, enabling murder with impunity. Ironically, as you steel yourself to encounter this book, the most difficult passage to read may be this description of California before contact. It seems like a fantasy at first. Inured by centuries of accounts from observers who didn't recognize resource management as farming or who dismissed complex oral literature as culture, we find the reality of a diverse, prosperous, well-populated homeland shocking. It brings the certain knowledge of what humankind has lost.

GHOST TOWN 1
BEFORE CONTACT

AN AMERICAN GENOCIDE:
THE UNITED STATES AND THE CALIFORNIA INDIAN CATASTROPHE, 1846–1873

BENJAMIN MADLEY

CALIFORNIA INDIANS BEFORE CONTACT

IN THE CENTURIES BEFORE EUROPEANS ARRIVED,

California Indians inhabited a world different from the California we know today. Rivers ran undammed to the Pacific, man-made lakes like the Salton Sea and Lake Shasta had yet to be imagined, and vast wetlands bordered many rivers and bays. Other bodies of water were far larger than they are today. Eastern California's now mostly dry Owens Lake covered more than 100 square miles, San Francisco Bay was almost a third larger, and the San Joaquin Valley's now vanished Tulare Lake was the largest body of fresh water west of the Mississippi.

The flora and fauna, in their variety and sheer abundance, would also be unrecognizable to twenty-first-century Californians. Antelope, deer, and elk surged through the vast grasslands of the Central Valley in large herds. Mountain lions and grizzly bears—the latter now extinct in the golden state—searched for food. Forests—far larger than today's and filled with huge, old-growth trees—teemed with animals while oak groves proliferated. Shellfish thronged tidal estuaries. Vast schools of fish navigated rivers and bays. Great flocks of gulls, pelicans, and seagulls wheeled overhead. In the open ocean, fish, whales, seals, and sea otters swam by the thousands along the coast. There were no megacities, freeways, or factory farms. Yet ancient civilizations marked the land.

From a plank house on the redwood coast came the dawn cries of a newborn Wiyot infant. Near the Sacramento River, Wintu people spoke quietly around the morning fire in their subterranean lodge. As the sun climbed, the yells of a Northern Paiute family drove rabbits into a corral of rocks and branches. At noon, the skis of a Washoe man hissed over dazzling snow high above Lake Tahoe, and in the parched Mojave, precious liquid trickled over a young Kawaiisu as she passed into womanhood by "bathing in a wild chrysanthemum solution." On Santa Rosa Island, off the southern coast, a Chumash man and woman bound themselves in marriage by eating from the same dish even as, to the east, conversations rose from the desert as Cahuilla potters fashioned carefully painted and delicately incised earthenware. Up and down California women gathered, as their mothers, grandmothers, and great-grandmothers had before them, to weave baskets bearing intricate designs, each particular to their community.

As night fell, people gathered to celebrate, pray, and give thanks in the sacred songs and dances of their many traditions.

California on the eve of contact with Europeans was an exuberant clamor of Native American economies, languages, tribes, and individuals. Indigenous people had worshipped, loved, traded, and fought in California for at least 12,000 years—some believe since time immemorial. A number of Southern California Indian peoples, such as the Quechans, farmed—mainly corn, beans, and squash—along the Colorado River. Yet most California Indians depended on carefully managing, harvesting, and processing nature's bounty. Almost everywhere, they modified and maintained their environments in order to maximize hunting and gathering yields. Ethnoecologist M. Kat Anderson has called these practices "tending the wild." California Indians consciously created anthropogenic environments—forests, groves, grasslands, and meadows—fashioned and managed over centuries through techniques that included pruning, tilling, sowing, selective harvesting, and, most important, burning.

Game provided vital components of many precontact California Indian diets and material cultures. Instead of domesticating animals, California Indians frequently modified their environments to increase antelope, bear, bird, deer, elk, rabbit, and other game populations. By selectively and repeatedly burning portions of their land to clear unwanted undergrowth and promote forage for herbivores, California Indians increased the number of herbivores as well as the population of carnivores who ate them, maximizing local game populations and thus their total game supply. These practices bore striking similarities to the ways in which some other Native Americans, elsewhere in North America, shaped and managed their local environments to suit their own needs.

As in other regions of North America, the results of such fire-based indigenous game-management programs deeply impressed early European visitors. These newcomers frequently expressed astonishment at the variety and sheer numbers of game animals in California before colonization. For example, in 1579, the Englishman Sir Francis Drake described how, at one point on the California coast, "infinite was the company of very large and fat Deere, which there we sawe by thousands, as we supposed, in a heard." In 1602, the Spaniard Juan Sebastián Vizcaíno wrote that in the Monterey area, "there is much wild game, such as harts, like young bulls, deer, buffalo, very large bears, rabbits, hares, and many other animals and many game birds, such as geese, partridges, quail, crane, ducks, vultures, and many other kinds of birds." Abundant animal populations formed a cornerstone of life for many indigenous Californians well into the second half of the nineteenth century.

California Indian hunters, usually men, developed a wide repertoire of local techniques and technologies to take game. For example, in the forested Klamath River region near the Oregon border, Karuks used dogs to drive elk into ravines. To the southeast, Atsugewis used deer-head disguises to closely approach, surprise, and take deer. In the mountains around Lake Tahoe, groups of Washoe men on snowshoes hunted deer and mountain sheep. Patwins in the southwestern Sacramento Valley deployed goose-skin-stuffed decoys while duck hunting, and Nisenan people, east of the Sacramento River, constructed net fences into which they drove and entangled rabbits before clubbing them. Farther south, San Joaquin Valley Southern Yokuts set underwater snares to capture geese, ducks, and other waterfowl, and, near what is now San Diego, Luiseños used a "curved throwing stick," or *wakut,* to hunt rabbits.

California Indians prepared and preserved the edible portions of the game that they killed in many ways, often using inedible portions for other purposes. Cooks frequently roasted meat simply, but some employed more elaborate preparations. The Konkow wrapped game in maple leaves before baking, Miwoks baked or steamed fresh meat, and Lake Miwoks cooked a mixture of pulverized rabbit bones and deer blood between leaves in the coals. California Indian people also preserved meat for future use with salt, sun, smoke, or some combination of the three. Particular tribes also ground dried meat and bone into meal. Beyond nourishment, game animals also provided a variety of materials important to traditional life, including buckskin and pelts for clothing, sinews for bows and bowstrings, feathers for regalia, and bones, horns, and hoofs for fashioning tools and making medicine.

Gathering, generally done by women, added to the richness and variety of California Indian diets. As with game, California Indians carefully managed their environments to maximize yields. They also employed multiple technologies to process harvests. Some California Indians constructed substantial earthen ovens to roast soaproot bulbs and cooked other foods by placing hot rocks into baskets so tightly woven that they held boiling water. Many California Indian peoples also removed the tannic acid from acorns (generally by grinding them into a powder, then soaking them before cooking) to create that staple of so many indigenous California diets: the acorn meal that could be used to make porridge, bake bread, and thicken soups. Gathering also provided additional important sources of protein and carbohydrates. Some California Indian peoples harvested energy-dense pine nuts from the foothills and mountains. In the meadows and valleys, people often gathered grass seeds, and, according to a Lassik/Wailaki woman, Lucy Young, "Grasshoppers were considered quite a delicacy" with their "sweet, buttery, nutty flavor." A wide variety of berries added nutrients and sweetness to California Indian diets. Some peoples crushed manzanita berries, placed them in a sieve, and poured cool water over them to make a sweet amber cider. Others brewed and drank fragrant Sierra mint tea. California Indians also saved gathered foods for future use or trade and sometimes stored them in granaries.

California's freshwater ecosystems provided another major source of nutrition, and California Indians used a wide range of methods to reap this bounty. The Hupa, Chilulua, and Whilkut peoples of northwestern California built weirs during low water in the fall to capture river fish. Others, like the Yanas east of the northern Sacramento River, speared fish in streams and pools. Wailakis in the Coast Range deployed nets "made from wild iris fibre," Modocs in the northeast fished from dugout pine shovel-nosed canoes, and the Tubatulabals of south central California built stone and willow-branch fish corrals and held communal fish drives.

To harvest marine species, some California Indians deployed other technologies. Tolowas near the Oregon border harpooned sea lions from oceangoing redwood canoes. Coast Miwoks north of San Francisco set fish traps, and Southern California's Chumash people constructed wooden plank boats—sometimes more than thirty feet long—from which they hunted seals, sea otters, and porpoises. Many California Indian peoples also harvested clams, mussels, and oysters along the coast and in tidal estuaries. They dried, smoked, or sometimes salted fish and seafood, wasting little. For example, the members of some tribes saved salmon bones and ground them into a nutritious powder that could be added to soups and stews. Preserved fish and seafood provided food in lean times and were also valuable trading commodities.

California's natural bounty, coupled with California Indians' ingenious ability to maximize and use that abundance, supported a population of perhaps 310,000 people before the arrival of Europeans. Thus, through environmental management, hunting, gathering, fishing, farming, and food processing, Indians created a California that may have been the most densely populated region north of Mexico in the years before Christopher Columbus first visited the Western Hemisphere.

These hundreds of thousands of people spoke a dazzling array of languages. Precontact North America was a diverse linguistic landscape. Indigenous peoples between the Rio Grande River and the Arctic Ocean spoke about 300 different languages that can be classified into more than fifty different language families. In contrast, linguists classify Europe's languages into as few as three families. Amid indigenous North America's already varied linguistic landscape, precontact California stands out as one of the most linguistically diverse places on earth. California Indians spoke perhaps one hundred separate languages, classified by linguists into at least five different language families, some "as mutually unintelligible as English and Chinese."

Speaking scores of languages, California Indians created dozens of cultural and political units. Anthropologists recognize at least sixty major tribes in California that can, in turn, be divided into many more linguistic and tribal subgroups. For example, anthropologists have classified the Pomo people north of San Francisco Bay into seven different subgroups and the Yana of the Southern Cascades into five subgroups. California's many subgroups can be divided further into about 500 individual bands, given that each village or village constellation tended to act as its own politically and economically autonomous entity. The indigenous peoples of California were thus highly independent but loosely bound to larger tribal groups by shared languages and cultures.

Systems of exchange also connected California Indian peoples to each

AN AMERICAN GENOCIDE

other and helped to distribute food, raw materials, manufactured goods, and luxuries. Theirs was a mixed economy in which dentalia, or seashell currency, often facilitated transactions within and beyond California. Traded foods included acorns, beans, berries, fish, meat, nuts, roots, salt, seafood, seaweed, and seeds. Traded raw materials included furs, hides, sinew, skins, and obsidian—a volcanic glass used to make knives, arrowheads, and other tools. California Indian people also exchanged manufactured goods. These included arrowheads, baskets, bows, cradle frames, moccasins, nets and snares, redwood canoes, rope, stone mortars and pestles, stone vessels, and buckeye fire drills for starting fires. Traded luxuries included tobacco and pipes, decorative woodpecker scalps, ornamental shell, carved nuts, and pigments.

California Indians did have violent conflicts with each other before contact with Europeans, but warfare does not seem to have dominated their lives. As early as 1875, ethnographer Stephen Powers remarked that California Indians "were not a martial race, but rather peaceable." More recently, anthropologists Robert Heizer and Albert Elsasser observed that "except for the Colorado River tribes, who placed a value on warfare, the California Indians were peaceable and unaggressive."

California before European contact was a thriving, staggeringly diverse place. Peoples speaking scores of different languages organized themselves into hundreds of political entities and connected themselves to each other via dense webs of local and regional cultural exchange while maintaining trading connections with peoples farther away. Their lifeways changed over the course of millennia, but the arrival of Europeans brought rapid, and for many tribes, catastrophic transformations.

Historians point out that California has a more extensive pool of memoirs and first-person accounts from the time of its Mexican rule than other Southwestern US regions. Partly this is because Hubert Howe Bancroft, whose 60,000-piece collection of books, maps, and manuscripts formed the nucleus of the Bancroft Library at the University of California, also collected the memories of living people. With the help of assistants, he began in the 1860s to interview pioneers, merchants, settlers, and prominent citizens about the recent, often tumultuous, past. The *testimonios* taken by Bancroft's assistants from Californios are today carefully scrutinized for accuracy, because practices at the time allowed for the "Dictations" to be edited and translated as they were written down and filtered in other ways, too. But sometimes in the middle of obviously prettied-up reminiscences, you'll come across a moment like this origin story of class-consciousness in L.A. Its eyewitness-account immediacy lets us quickly see through the social attitudes of the wealthy Spaniard and the romanticizing translator.

STONER PARTY

A MEMOIR

MEMOIRS OF A MERCHANT

JOSÉ ARNAZ,

TRANSLATED BY NELLIE VAN DE GRIFT SANCHEZ

THE CALIFORNIANS WERE GENERALLY FOND OF diversions, above all, of balls and bull-fights. Society, at the time of my arrival in Los Angeles, was mixed, rich and poor, honorable women and otherwise. About this time an effort was being made to establish a circle of decent and honorable people. In fact, on the 16th of September, 1840, there were two public balls held, one in the plaza under an arbor, which was attended by the greater part of the populace and the common people. The other, given at the house of Abel Stearns, was attended by the most prominent members of the population, who came by invitation. In order to protect this function, a guard was placed at the door as a measure of precaution, but even this did not prevent the people, angered at seeing themselves treated with contempt, from throwing stones and breaking the windows in Stearns' house—an occurrence that was never repeated. From that time two sets of society were established in Los Angeles, without further interruption, the house of Señor Stearns being the center of the select circle.

PHOTO BY HARTMUT WALTER

Ethereal yellow clouds of flowering mustard along our coastal highways make it one of L.A.'s favorite long-naturalized non-native plants, but in fact the people you might see foraging in mustard fields today are after the leaves (one of those "healthy greens"). It wasn't always so. In the latter half of the nineteenth century, farmers and others recently arrived in the now-American state looked on California mustard as a potential cash crop for its abundant seed (unlike the rancheros, for whom its vast stands had been a pasture-destroying pest). Few of us have heard anything of the history of the effort by inventors in the late 1800s to come up with an efficient way to turn all that "volunteer" mustard into a viable product. But mechanization can't solve every challenge.

NATURE NOTE 1
WEED SEED

HARVESTING WILD MUSTARD

H.E. LOUGHEED

UNTIL THE EIGHTIES, SOUTHERN CALIFORNIA WAS A LAND OF mustard fields. The plant was indigenous to the country, and in the days before the gas engine, it encroached upon the hayfields to such an extent, it was considered a pest by the ranchers. It was hard to get rid of, and many a ton of hay was well spiced with the dry stalks that held no enticement for stock. Hayfields and wild mustard—and the mustard fields were much larger than the hayfields. And sheep! There were thousands upon thousands of them in what is now the metropolitan area of Los Angeles.

Great fields of mustard extended from the outskirts of the then-Los Angeles city limits east and south—through Alhambra, El Monte, and the Puente districts; Whittier and Santa Fe Springs (then known as Fulton Wells); and the San Pedro and Redondo areas.

The plant varied in height, according to the dryness or wetness of the seasons—from four to six feet, to eight to ten feet. It was a beautiful sight in the spring of the year, literally miles of yellow bloom overshadowing the green of the stalks and leaves.

My father, Joseph Lougheed, arrived in the late 1850s. He marveled at the sight. Mustard was used on the table and in mustard plasters. It made a fine grade of oil, and it was said that the brown hulls were used to adulterate pepper. Why couldn't some method be found to harvest it? At that time a number of Chinese were gathering it with hand sickles. It was a slow process, but they made good wages; the seed sold for eight to fifteen cents a pound.

After several years in Southern California, Dad went to San Francisco. But mustard was on his mind. He drew plans for a harvester that he thought might work and had machinery built at the Union Iron Works.

In 1874 he came back to Los Angeles with his family and bought a ten-acre ranch on the old Wilmington Road, now known as Avalon Boulevard. As time permitted from his farm duties, he worked on his header, and in 1876 he tried it out in a large field of mustard on the old Wilmington Road, about where Fifty-Sixth Street now crosses it.

But the header wouldn't work. The centers of mustard stalks are pithy, and they clogged and stopped the knife. That season was a failure, but Dad kept tinkering. He did away with the cutting knife and rigged the reel so that it whirled rapidly and broke off the brittle stalks. So far so good. But too much seed was wasted. The flying reel scattered it in all directions. For when the seed is ripe, the pods slowly begin to open to the afternoon breeze.

More tinkering was to be done. A half-dozen other men were also trying to develop a machine that would successfully gather the seed. Finally, all except Dad gave it up.

The machine he finally evolved gathered most of the seed. Troughs, pointed at the front end, eight inches wide, six inches deep, and five feet long, spaced two inches apart, projected from the front of the header. The mustard stalks were crowded through the spaces between the troughs and broken off by the flying reel. The troughs caught a great deal of seed, but most of it, along with the stalks and chaff, was thrown into the box behind the reel. The box was an integral part of the header, the same width and about ten feet deep. It was covered over with canvas to contain the flying seed. Inside a man pitched out the stalks through an opening that was made for this purpose. It was a dirty job. The worker had to wear goggles, and to further protect his face from the flying seed, a twelve-inch board was slung behind the reel. The seed hitting this fell to the floor.

The box when full held fifty grain sacks of chaff and seed. The driver and worker inside then sacked it and stacked it in the field where the camp wagon picked it up.

Had Dad been in operation ten or fifteen years earlier, he might have made a modest fortune. But by the time he got into successful operation, the price of seed had dropped to two to four cents a pound. This drop in price may have been due to the fact that English mustard was beginning to be raised around Lompoc, thus increasing supply over demand.

At any rate, Dad kept going, and some years he did pretty well. He built a second header. And every spring at blossom time he hitched a horse to the buggy and drove over the country, inspecting the fields to determine the best location for the season's operations. And again, before the seed was ripe, he would journey forth to see how the crop was progressing.

The middle of June usually saw camp set up and harvesting begun. Seldom was camp moved during a season, for the fields were so great, the work could be economically accomplished from the one stand. The season lasted from six to eight weeks. There were plenty of fields left after that period, but there wasn't enough seed left in the pods to make harvesting pay.

In the dry years, when the mustard stalks were shorter and thinner, six horses were enough for each header. But after a wet winter, when there was a rank growth, eight horses were required. Sometimes a field was so infested with red-winged blackbirds' nests that the flying reel would become completely clogged. The load would become so heavy that the attaching belt to the bull wheel would slip and the reel stop. There was nothing to do but lay to and clean up the mess. This particular trouble occurred chiefly in the El Monte area.

The Redondo section brought other troubles. It was impossible to operate the headers on a fog-wet morning, as then the mustard stalks were not brittle and the reel couldn't break them off. Sometimes it was ten or eleven o'clock before the crew got to work. Fortunately, this didn't occur often.

Another difficulty was the hard adobe ground. Much of it had never seen a plow, and the cracks, here and there, were so wide that the tiller wheel dropped into them and sometimes snapped off.

And old wells were far from uncommon. They supplied the water for the thousands of sheep the country supported. But when a well ran dry, the mustard soon engulfed the old well and it was impossible to see. A wheel of a machine occasionally slipped into one of the half-buried wells. Not much damage was done, but it would take several hours to dig out.

After the sacked seed was brought to camp, it was separated from the chaff. In the afternoons when there was a breeze, the sacks were dumped onto a screen slung below two cross bars between upright posts. This screen was five feet wide by ten feet long, with eight-inch wooden sides. It was swung vigorously back and forth, the seed dropping to a sheet of canvas, the lighter chaff being worked over the lower end.

The seed, too small to be contained in burlap bags, was then scooped into muslin sacks made expressly for the purpose. It was fairly clean but had still to go through another process. In the mornings when there was no breeze, it was put through a fanning mill. It came out of this absolutely clean and ready for market. It was shipped to commission merchants, sometimes to San Francisco, sometimes to New York, depending upon the market.

The largest output of any season was 1,100 sacks, averaging ninety-five pounds to the sack. At four cents a pound, it brought good money. In those days horses were hired for twenty-five cents a day, including harness. But when seed was selling at two cents, the take was small.

Most of the ranchers were glad to have the mustard headers work over their land. It left less seed to sprout the following year. Harvesting several seasons over the same field thinned it out to such an extent that a farmer could raise a fair crop of hay. But there was one big concern that didn't believe in giving anything away, even a pest, and charged five cents a sack for the privilege of harvesting their lands.

But the country began to change. Water was being developed. More land was being put under cultivation. Orchards were springing up, and the sheep were disappearing. The mustard fields were shrinking, 'til it was hard to find acreage enough for a season's harvesting.

It was about 1890 that Dad took his last trip in the spring to look over the fields. He shook his head. Not enough to bother with, he thought. And so the harvesting of wild mustard ended.

PHOTO BY ANN SUMMA

When *Paperback L.A.* senses a gap in the popular history record of our town, we often know just where to turn for answers. In this case, we got to wondering what happened to car manufacturing, which we knew had been a thing in L.A. in the late nineteenth and very early twentieth centuries. So we asked automotive journalist Preston Lerner, who explained that L.A.'s most important contributions to "car culture" weren't convertibles or, for that matter, drive-ins with roller-skating waitresses. No, when it comes to car history, L.A. has been all about exuberant speed and exuberant design. L.A.'s monumental importance to auto racing and other motorsports has rarely gotten the attention it deserves, which is why we lose sight of the big story when we wonder, "Whatever happened to that raceway we went to when I was a kid?" or "What was that Jan and Dean song?" Now, Lerner has pulled all the strands together in this definitive timeline. Take *this* to your car-club meeting and win a few arguments.

CAR CRAZY
A TIMELINE

HOT, FAST, AND DANGEROUS

PRESTON LERNER

POP QUIZ: WHAT WAS THE FIRST CAPITAL OF THE AMERICAN automobile racing industry? No, not Detroit. Not even Indianapolis. Try Los Angeles. Yes, prosaic street cars were cranked out by the million in the Midwest. But Southern California offered idyllic weather, wide-open spaces, and the daredevil gene, and go-fast types from all over the country made pilgrimages here to worship at the altar of Harry Miller, the great engineering genius of the Roaring Twenties, and race on legendary tracks like Ascot Legion Speedway. The Southland was the cradle of hot-rod civilization, which spawned not only drag racing but also the kustom-car, street-rod, and rat-rod cultures. And while one rogue strand of SoCal need-for-speed DNA led to the invention of off-road racing, another gave birth to the rice-rocket craze (and *The Fast and the Furious* movie franchise). Even the lowly go-kart was a made-in-L.A. phenomenon. Rising real estate values and not-in-my-backyard concerns doomed most local tracks in the eighties and nineties, and Southern California lost much of its racing mojo. But if Los Angeles is no longer a motorsports mecca, it still boasts a richer racing heritage than any American city other than Indianapolis.

1907 – Harry Arminius Miller, the colossus of early American motorsports, sets up shop in downtown Los Angeles to build his patented high-performance carburetors.

1909 – One month before the first race at the Indianapolis Motor Speedway, the inaugural Santa Monica Road Race is held on an 8.4-mile circuit incorporating Ocean Avenue, Nevada Avenue—now known as Wilshire Boulevard—and San Vicente Boulevard. An Apperson Jack Rabbit wins the race at an average speed of 64.44 miles per hour.

1910 – Southern California's first purpose-built racetrack, the Los Angeles Motordrome, opens in Playa del Rey. Headliner Barney Oldfield is outrun in the headline event by Caleb Bragg, a high-society millionaire from Pasadena. When a fire destroys the extremely fast and dangerous track three years later, newspaper columnist Damon Runyon writes trenchantly, "Playa del Rey burned down last night, with great savings of lives."

1920 – Harry Miller moves to 2625 Long Beach Avenue and begins building some of the most advanced and iconic race cars of the twentieth century. Slender, jewel-like Millers set standards for performance, engineering ingenuity, and irrational beauty. Working with right hand man Leo Goossen, Miller unlocks technical secrets ranging from supercharging to front-wheel drive, and his factory transforms L.A. into the center of American racing for decades to come. To this day, Millers are venerated as aesthetic and technological masterpieces.

1923 – Construction of Mulholland Highway starts. When it opens the following year, it quickly emerges as a de facto, if illegal, racetrack for local speed demons.

1924 – The final race is held at the magnificent board track—a 1.25-mile banked oval fashioned out of 300 miles of wood two-by-fours—that had been erected in the heart of Beverly Hills four years earlier. Fourteen of the seventeen entries are Millers. (The rest are Duesenbergs.) The winner averages 116.6 miles per hour for the 200-lap race.

1926 – L.A.-raised, self-taught engineer Frank Lockhart—a real-life precursor to the radio character Jack Armstrong, the All-American Boy—goes to the Indianapolis 500 as a relief driver, with no experience racing on anything but dirt tracks. He is permitted to race only after another driver gets sick. He then laps the field—twice!—en route to winning the Indy 500 in a Miller. Two years later, while chasing the land-speed record in an innovative car he designed and built himself, he dies after crashing at 225 miles per hour on the sand at Daytona Beach, Florida.

1928 – George Wight builds a brick building near his junkyard in Bell and begins selling "speed" equipment stripped off moribund cars to do-it-yourselfers looking to upgrade the performance of their Model T Fords. Bell Auto Parts is the nation's first speed shop and a necessary precursor to the coming hot-rod revolution.

1931 – Dan Gurney, who will move to Southern California and become the postwar reincarnation of Frank Lockhart (see 1926, above), is born in Port Jefferson, New York.

1933 – After Harry Miller goes bankrupt, a victim of the Great Depression, his former shop foreman, Fred Offenhauser, hangs out his own shingle in Mid-City and starts building powerful yet nearly indestructible four-cylinder motors based on an old Miller marine engine. These Offys, as they are dubbed, go on to dominate American racing for nearly half a century. Miller takes several more shots at winning Indy, once in concert with star-crossed promotor Preston Tucker, but all of these late-life adventures end badly.

1936 – Legion Ascot Speedway closes after a driver and his riding mechanic crash fatally in front of a crowd of 35,000. A nationally renowned five-eighths-mile dirt oval, located in the hills east of Lincoln Heights, Ascot is run by American Legion Post 127 of nearby Glendale. It is known as the Killer Track because so many people die there. Eight months after the track is padlocked, the grandstands are destroyed in a mysterious fire. Years later, a former janitor confesses to committing arson. "I thought maybe they might reopen it and kill some more of my friends," he says. "So I decided to burn the grandstand down."

1937 – Although the term "hot rodding" has not yet been coined, a group of soon-to-be-called hot rodders forms the Southern California Timing Association. The next year, the SCTA stages its first speed meet, at Muroc Dry Lake in the Mojave Desert.

HOT, FAST, AND DANGEROUS

1940 – Arroyo Seco Parkway, now known as the Pasadena Freeway, becomes the state's first freeway. With its relatively sharp and lightly banked turns, the road is soon something of a municipal racetrack.

1945 – Even before the war with Japan ends, Frank Kurtis takes orders for ten midgets—essentially, Indy cars writ small—at his shop in Glendale. Able to run on small, tight tracks that make for nonstop action, midgets are immensely popular during the postwar era, and Kurtis-Kraft rides the wave to become the world's most prolific race car manufacturer. Besides selling 550 ready-to-race midgets and kits for 600 more, Kurtis also builds hundreds of full-size open-wheel racers, sports cars, and dragsters that win five Indy 500s and countless other races.

1947 – The California Sports Car Club holds its first race, a hill climb in Palos Verdes.

1948 – Pete Petersen sells the first issues of *Hot Rod* magazine for 25 cents a pop on the steps of the Los Angeles National Guard Armory at the SCTA's First Annual Hot Rod Exposition. It would be difficult to overstate the influence SoCal car magazines such as *Hot Rod*, *Road & Truck*, and *Motor Trend* have on the nascent car enthusiast market. Known in the trade as buff books, they not only spread the gospel but also help define the culture. In 1996, Petersen sells his publishing empire for $450 million. But the early days are a struggle. "We'd be at a drive-in or a race, and we'd say, 'Let's go sell some subs,'" Petersen says, recalling when subscriptions were a mere $3 a year. "We'd sell 'em, then we'd have enough money for supper."

1948 – The first Ferrari imported to the United States is bought by Tommy Lee, scion of a Southern California car dealership and radio station fortune.

1948 – After graduating from high school, Dan Gurney moves to Riverside and hones his driving skills by racing through orange groves.

1949 – Santa Monica's Phil Hill enters and wins his first race in an MG TC, at Carrell Speedway in Gardena. Built near the site of Ascot Legion, Carrell is the backdrop for the Mickey Rooney film *The Big Wheel*, which is an early entry on a long list of nearly unwatchable cliché-ridden movies about racing.

1950 – Gas station owner C.J. "Pappy" Hart opens the first professional drag strip on an unused runway at Orange County Airport. He also establishes the general drag racing principles used to this day—a quarter-mile-long race from a standing start between two side-by-side participants. Admission to the Santa Ana Drags, as it is unofficially but universally known, is 50 cents whether you are a spectator or a racer.

1951 – Wally Parks, the first editor of *Hot Rod* and the single most important figure in hot-rod history, founds the National Hot Rod Association. In an effort to stop illegal street racing, the NHRA embarks on a nationwide drag racing program for amateurs and professionals. The first NHRA-sanctioned event is held two years later in the parking lot of the Los Angeles County Fairgrounds in Pomona. Hot rods were—and still are—expressions of personal style, unconstrained by formal rules. But Parks is a straight arrow who becomes revered as the patriarch of drag racing for bringing what had been an outlaw sport into mainstream society.

1953 – Brothers George and Sam Barris create the Hirohata Merc, a nosed, decked, shaved, and chopped 1951 Mercury Club Coupe that becomes one of the foundational documents of the kustom-car movement. Later, the voluble George Barris, a consummate showman, is immortalized in Tom Wolfe's famous *Esquire* piece (and title story of a subsequent book) "The Kandy-Kolored Tangerine-Flake Streamline Baby." Working out of a shop in North Hollywood, Barris is best known for made-for-TV creations such as the original Batmobile and the Munster Koach.

1954 – Alhambra native Mickey Thompson, an *L.A. Times* pressman by trade, unveils the world's first purpose-built dragster. It is dubbed a "slingshot" because the cockpit is at the tail of the car, behind the rear axle. The protean Thompson goes on to become one of the most influential and polarizing figures in American motorsports through his involvement in Indy car racing, land-speed-record racing, and off-road racing.

1955 – James Dean is killed near Cholame, California, while driving his Porsche 550 Spyder, nicknamed "Little Bastard," from Competition Motors in Hollywood to a race in Salinas.

1955 – Dan Gurney makes his racing debut in a Triumph TR2 in a Torrey Pines road race.

1956 – Art Ingels, a fabricator at Kurtis-Kraft, cobbles together the world's first go-kart out of surplus tubing and a two-stroke lawn mower engine in a garage in Echo Park and tests it in the parking lot of the Rose Bowl.

1957 – Riverside International Raceway opens and is hailed as the premier road course in the country. Meanwhile, amateur racer Bob Drake opens the Grand Prix Restaurant on Beverly Boulevard, and it becomes a favorite haunt of bench racers throughout Southern California.

1958 – The NHRA implements its notorious Nitro Ban—outlawing the use of nitroglycerine as a fuel additive—to cap speeds that had soared past 160 miles per hour. But fans prefer the tear-inducing spectacle of nitro-powered cars and never fully embrace the notion of gasoline-only drag racing. So Wally Parks lifts the ban in 1963, and today's Top Fuel rails and Funny Cars routinely trip the timing lights at more than 300 miles per hour.

1959 – Every car in the Indy 500 is powered by an Offenhauser engine, and virtually every chassis is built either at Kurtis-Kraft or at one of a half dozen other race shops in L.A.

1960 – In a home-built racer powered by not one, not two, not three but *four* supercharged Pontiac V-8s, Mickey Thompson blasts across the Bonneville Salt Flats at 406.60 miles per hour. He fails to set a new land-speed record, however, because his car, Challenger I, breaks before he can "back up" his speed with the required second run.

1961 – Driving a shark-nosed Ferrari, Phil Hill wins the Italian Grand Prix at Monza to claim the Formula 1 World Driving Championship. The previous year, also at Monza, Hill had become the first American to win a European Grand Prix since Jimmy Murphy—who also grew up in Southern California—won the French Grand Prix in 1921. The only other American F1 World Champion is Italian native Mario Andretti.

1962 – Carroll Shelby starts building hairy-chested, Ford-powered Cobra roadsters in the shop in Venice where an all-star team of Southern Californian hot rodders and road racers amassed by Lance Reventlow, the son of Woolworth heiress Barbara Hutton, had created the all-conquering Scarab sports cars.

1963 – The Beach Boys record "Little Deuce Coupe." ("She's ported and relieved, and she's stroked and bored. She'll do a hundred and forty with the top end floored.") The next year, Jan and Dean, not to be outdone, release "The Little Old Lady (From Pasadena)." ("She drives real fast, and she drives real hard. She's the terror of Colorado Boulevard.")

1964 – Dave MacDonald, an El Monte wunderkind who earned his reputation driving Cobras for Carroll Shelby, dies in a fireball during the Indy 500. The hellish accident, which also kills a second driver, causes the race to be stopped for nearly two hours. MacDonald was driving a radical, evil-handling car—derisively dubbed a "superskate"—created by Mickey Thompson.

1965 – Craig Breedlove, a graduate of Venice High School, sets the land-speed record at Bonneville for the fifth and final time, at 600.601 miles per hour in a jet-turbine-powered projectile called the "Spirit of America." During a previous run, he'd lost control at 500 miles per hour, scythed through a telephone pole, flew over a dike, and nosed into the water. "And now for my next act, I'm going to set myself on fire," he'd joked afterward.

1967 – The precursor to the Baja 1000 is run in Mexico for the first time, from Tijuana to La Paz, marking the invention of off-road racing. The winning vehicle is a dune buggy based on the VW Beetle known as the Meyers Manx, a seminal vehicle designed and built by a kamikaze attack survivor–turned–beach bum named Bruce Meyers in a garage in Newport Beach.

1967 – Dan Gurney scores what's often considered the most remarkable double in racing history. On June 11, he and co-driver A.J. Foyt wheel a Ford GT Mark IV to victory in the 24 Hours of Le Mans. The next Sunday, Gurney wins the Belgian Grand Prix in a beak-nosed Eagle built at his shop, All American Racers, in Santa Ana. This is the first—and last—Formula 1 victory scored by an American car. Tall and handsome, with a sunny Southern California disposition and an all-American smile, Gurney is among the greatest race car personalities ever produced by the United States, and he is perhaps the most widely admired. Which is why, in 1964, *Car and Driver* conducted a fanciful Dan Gurney for President campaign. (Bumper stickers are still available on eBay.)

1968 – The first Hot Wheels model cars are unveiled by Mattel, to tremendous acclaim. Most of them are designed by Harry Bradley, a transportation design professor at the Art Center College in downtown L.A. Bradley later designs a Wienermobile for Oscar Mayer.

1970 – Don "The Snake" Prudhomme, who grew up working in his family's body shop in Burbank, barnstorms around the country in a series of winner-takes-all drag races against Tom "The Mongoose" McEwen. Each of them runs what is known as a Funny Car—a purpose-built, tube-frame dragster with a fiberglass body that resembles a street car—sponsored by Hot Wheels. By marrying horsepower with carnival hype and pro-wrestling-style bluster, the high-profile Snake-and-Mongoose show ratchets up national interest in drag racing and injects serious money into the sport for the first time.

1971 – Steve McQueen produces and stars in *Le Mans*, which is at once the greatest racing movie ever made and one of the most banal films ever released. It bankrupts his company, Solar Productions, named after the street where he lived in the Hollywood Hills. But it produces one memorable quote: "When you're racing, it's life. Anything that happens before or after is just waiting."

1972 – Jerry Grant breaks the 200-miles-per hour barrier in an Eagle Indy car at Ontario Motor Speedway. The next year, Gurney Eagles finishes 1-2 in the Indy 500 and accounts for more than half the cars in the field.

1975 – Travel agent Chris Pook convinces civic leaders that they can create a SoCal version of the Monaco Grand Prix by staging a street race in Long Beach. Skeptics point out that the Long Beach waterfront features dive bars and X-rated movie theaters rather than yachts and a casino. But against all odds, the Long Beach Grand Prix is a knockout. Besides fueling upscale development in Long Beach, Pook's extravaganza launches dozens of other street races all over the world—including, briefly, one in downtown L.A. But other than Monaco, none is more popular or prestigious than the annual bash in Long Beach.

1978 – The California Jam II rock concert at Ontario Motor Speedway is a gigantic success—and it dooms the track. Built in 1970, Ontario is a carbon copy of the Indianapolis Motor Speedway. The ownership group includes the South Bay's Parnelli Jones, who'd won the Indy 500 in 1963 in a car owned by legendary Los Angeles race promoter J.C. Agajanian. The track had trouble drawing fans to races, so the owners staged the California Jam extravaganza— headlined by Deep Purple—in 1974 to bring in more money. Four years later, 350,000 fans flock to Ontario to see Aerosmith, Foreigner, and Rush et al at Cal Jam II. But concertgoers trash the neighborhood so thoroughly that civic leaders turn against the track, and it closes two years later.

1979 – Mickey Thompson moves off-road racing from the desert to the city and stages a closed-course race—complete with death-defying jumps fashioned out of 500 truckloads of dirt—inside the Los Angeles Coliseum. This Off-Road Grand Prix launches the new sport of stadium truck racing.

1980 – An Offy races in the Indy 500 for the last time. At least one engine based on the designs of Harry Miller has been at Indy every year going back to 1921.

1981 – *King of the Mountain*, a B movie starring Harry Hamlin, focuses on street racing on Mulholland Drive.

1988 – Mickey Thompson and his wife, Trudy, are murdered by two hooded gunmen outside their home near Monrovia. It isn't until 2001 that Thompson's estranged business partner, Michael Goodwin, is charged with murder. Six years later, Goodwin is convicted and sentenced to two consecutive counts of life without parole.

1989 – CadZZilla, a 1948 Cadillac Sedanette transformed into a long, luscious, ground-scraping custom by Boyd Coddington for ZZ Top front man Billy Gibbons, establishes a new model for street rodding. A onetime machinist at Disneyland, Coddington works out of a shop in Stanton. There, wearing his trademark Hawaiian shirts, he creates cost-no-object hot rods for well-heeled customers who want dramatic looks along with high-end build quality and creature comforts. Coddington's cars, full of gleaming components milled out of aluminum billet, are the polar opposites of the homemade contraptions that have defined hot rodding for decades.

1990 – The last race is run at Ascot Park in Gardena. Not to be confused with Ascot Legion (see 1936 entry), Ascot Park—whose most famous promoter is J.C. Agajanian—is a grubby half-mile oval built on a former dump site. Billed as the busiest dirt track in the country, it draws racers ranging from Mario Andretti to Dale Earnhardt, and it hosts the first public motorcycle jump by Evel Knievel. Agajanian's long-running radio pitch "Come to Ascot, where the 110, the 405, and the 91 freeways collide!" lives on.

1992 – The Moreno Valley Mall opens on the site of Riverside International Raceway, which had closed three years earlier.

1997 – A group led by motorsports powerhouse Roger Penske opens a two-mile superspeedway in Fontana on what had been the site of a steel mill (famously used as a location in *The Terminator*). More than 80,000 fans show up for its first major race, featuring NASCAR's gaudily colored, ground-shaking stock cars. Now known as Auto Club Speedway, the track is still an annual stop on the NASCAR schedule.

1999 – *Hot Rod Deluxe* magazine debuts and showcases the rat-rod culture emerging in Southern California to the rest of the country. Developed as an antidote to what critics consider the excess of Boyd Coddington–style street rods, rat rods are a return to the do-it-yourself roots of the hobby. Although some rat rods are crappy, if not outright dangerous, they embody a fresh contrarian attitude that prizes authenticity over comfort or conventional beauty. The rat-rod world also embraces tattoos, rockabilly, and an in-your-face ethos that attract a new generation to hot rodding. The original *Hot Rod Deluxe* folds after only two issues, but rat rods and the culture it inspired are still going strong.

2001 – *The Fast and the Furious*, a seemingly throwaway action movie about street racing in Los Angeles, unexpectedly becomes a breakout hit. Besides turning Vin Diesel into a star, the movie spawns seven sequels, with no end in sight. *The Fast and the Furious* also showcases the SoCal import-racer craze. Old-school hot rodders despise the import racers—who are largely Asian—calling them "ricers" and belittling their modifications of prosaic Hondas and Toyotas for speed and style. But the fast-and-the-furious types are doing exactly what hot rodders have always done, just starting with different cars.

2003 – The first drift event in the United States is held at Irwindale Speedway. In drifting, a motorsports version of figure skating imported from Japan, participants are judged on their ability to slide their cars sideways while generating vast clouds of tire smoke. Although purists are still perplexed by the phenomenon, drifting is the perfect expression of one definition of racing—turning money into noise.

2006 – The indefatigable John Force, a whirlwind who can talk nearly as fast as he can drive, clinches his fourteenth Funny Car championship during the NHRA Finals at Pomona. Since then, three of his daughters have won professional drag races en route to creating a unique motorsports dynasty, while Force himself is up to sixteen titles and counting.

2011 – Work begins at All American Racers on the DeltaWing, a Le Mans prototype that's the most radical race car of its generation. By this time, AAR has largely gotten out of the race car business in favor of making components for the aerospace industry. But Dan Gurney chooses to take on the project because the DeltaWing appeals to his love of innovation.

2012 – *Road & Track*, the country's oldest car-enthusiast magazine, moves to Michigan. Founded in 1947, *R&T* was originally published in New York City. But the mag moved to Playa del Rey in 1952 and then to Newport Beach in 1959. For decades, it was housed in a two-story, midcentury masterpiece designed by local architect Bill Ficker. One year after the publication was bought by the Hearst publishing empire, the entire staff was axed, and *R&T* quit Southern California for greener—or, at least, cheaper—pastures in Ann Arbor.

2013 – Paul Walker, a Glendale native who has been the yin to Vin Diesel's yang in *The Fast and the Furious* movies, dies in a crash in Valencia while riding as a passenger in a Porsche Carrera GT supercar. At the time, Walker was in the middle of filming *Furious 7*. He was forty years old.

2016 – Danny Thompson sets a land-speed class record of 406.7 miles per hour at Bonneville in a 5,000-horsepower version of the Challenger 2—the car his father, Mickey, had built in 1968 but never got a chance to run on the salt.

2018 – Dan Gurney, who has been the face of American racing for nearly six decades, dies from complications from pneumonia. The "Big Eagle" was eighty-six.

Hollywood's Children, published in 1979, offered readers a unique window into Hollywood's labor practices of the 1920s and '30s. Read today, it not only captures a less-seen view of the golden age of the studio system (from the perspective of working-class families for whom Hollywood meant survival), but with its gentle tone and vivid specifics, also reminds us that the exploitation of children in entertainment continues. Author Diana Serra Cary, the popular child star Baby Peggy of the silent era, draws on the stories of her famous antecedents and shares her own memories of terrifying dangers on set and her crippling guilt as an unemployed preteen. Now ninety-nine, Cary sees actress Baby Peggy, who began working full-time at the age of twenty months, as a different self, a former self. As an adult, she has advocated for child performers through her books and her work with Paul Petersen and the nonprofit A Minor Consideration.

BUSY TODDLER TESTIMONIAL

HOLLYWOOD'S CHILDREN:
AN INSIDE ACCOUNT OF THE CHILD STAR ERA
DIANA SERRA CARY

WHEN I WAS INTRODUCED TO MY NEW EMPLOYERS,

Julius Stern's first concern was to ask, "Is she housebroken?" Being assured I was, he took me in his arms for our first publicity still. Julius was a bland, oval-faced man, with shrewd eyes, a high forehead, a prominent nose, and a puckish smile. Like his brother, Abe, he was never without a derby (de rigueur in California from October to May) or a straw hat (May to October) clamped firmly on his head. Both brothers favored stripes, worked in shirtsleeves most of the time, and dressed up this undress with a high collar, a tie, and sleeve garters.

The Sterns had a good sense of what was funny on film, and some of their two-reelers ranked among the best ever made in that golden era of comedy. But they possessed little sense of what might seem ridiculous about themselves. In consequence, both men are among the most quoted pioneer figures in Hollywood. Julius is said to be that producer who was trying to coin a catchy name for his studio and an equally good slogan to go with it. Hitting upon the logo Miracle Pictures, he came up with: "If it's a good picture, it's a miracle!" No one could convince him it was a bad choice. When a competitor referred jokingly to the quality of the Stern brothers' slapstick two-reelers, Abe burst out indignantly, "Century comedies are not to be laughed at!" And when one of my directors wanted to go to a distant mountain location because the story called for spectacular scenery, Julius delivered the oft-quoted "A rock's a rock. A tree's a tree. Shoot it in Griffith Park!"

Century ran a weekly one-column ad in *The Saturday Evening Post* announcing its forthcoming films over the signature of its distributor, Carl Laemmle. "Look for Baby Peggy" read a classic example of pure Sterness. "She is only three years old, but she is a better actress than a lot of older people who draw aristocratic salaries. Exhibitors are booking her right and left; and there isn't a pretentious theater in the country that doesn't regard her as a great drawing card." My own aristocratic salary, paid to me by one of the least pretentious studios in the industry, later became a bone of contention, but at the beginning everyone was happy.

The studio maintained its own menagerie, for Julius, always fretful of the budget, reasoned that it was cheaper to keep his four-legged stars and extras in pens and cages scattered about the lot than it was to hire them by the day from such competitors as Gay's Lion Farm. Reading from the bottom up, in order of their earning power and popularity, were two toothless old lions, a mangy tiger, one brown bear in fair condition, a billy goat, several aging deer, a hoary old elephant called Charley, Teddy, a dignified Great Dane, Brownie the Wonder Dog, and an exceptionally ugly, clever, and world-famous chimpanzee, Joe Martin. Joe's yellow-toothed grin was his trademark; he starred in his own two-reelers and enjoyed a box-office following that many a human comedian of the day might have envied. He sometimes appeared in comedies with me, but usually he was too busy working on his own, for which I was secretly grateful, for I dreaded working with Joe.

The trainer for the tiger, the lions, the chimp, and the elephant was a muscular blond man named Curley Stecker. Although he was said to have an explosive temper when aroused, Stecker seemed good-natured enough, was a veteran animal handler, and got on well with most of his charges.

"But I hate working with old Charley," Stecker confided one day to Father and me when we met in the hayloft of the old barn overlooking the elephant's corral at the far end of the lot. We had chosen the loft as a quiet place to work on my diction. Although my films were silent, I nevertheless had to learn my lines, and Father had no patience with my childish lisping. As he plunged his pitchfork into the hay and tossed samplings down into Charley's corral, Stecker continued: "Old Charley turned on me once, some twenty years ago, and I had to beat him off with a chain. He never forgot it. Mrs. Stecker can work with him just as easy as she does with the big cats and Joe Martin.

But he'll have no part of me."

He leaned on his pitchfork, looking down as Charley lifted wisps of hay into his mouth with his trunk. "I always make it a point to throw him his hay from up here, or over the gate into his stockade. He don't like me inside, and when I have to go in, I always carry that." He pointed to a high-powered elephant gun leaning against the wall. After we left the loft, Father cautioned me never to go near Charley's pen alone. I hardly needed his warning, for everyone at Century harbored a secret fear that the elephant would one day break out of his corral and run amok across the lot.

If Julius kept animals against the day when the script rained tigers, in the prop department he hoarded enough scenery and supplies to film the history of the world. The big old building probably was not as vast as it seemed to me as a child, but it was crammed with painted flats of jungles, drawing rooms, palaces, and dungeons. There were jury boxes, gallows, pulpits and thrones, moose heads, cigar store Indians, African shields, carriage harnesses, medieval suits of armor, bits and pieces of castles, a drawbridge, sedan chairs—literally everything and anything that might be needed to simulate a fairly believable background on an unbelievably low budget. Every item in the prop department was familiar to me, too, for sooner or later nearly every weapon in this great arsenal of optical illusion found its way into one of the hundred and more Baby Peggy comedies that streamed off the studio assembly line on the average of one a week during my tenure at Century.

High above the working set, like giant yellow tulips in a black window box, bloomed the spots, big and little, on short stems and tall. The electricians who tended them seemed shadow people, raising and lowering the spots according to orders from below. If the first instruction I received was not to look into the camera, the second must have been to keep my eyes closed while they were setting up the lights. (Stand-ins came much later, and they never came to Century.)

Perhaps reflecting the stigma attached to retakes at Century, I soon developed into a quick study. Overhearing myself referred to by a director as "one-take Peggy" was more rewarding to me than all the effusive praise and adulation poured out upon me by visitors to the studio. From the outset, I understood that these people were "outsiders" who did not know me at all. It especially distressed and embarrassed me to see older and otherwise very dignified bank presidents and politicians reduced to doting grandparents by a little girl who was, in fact, a total stranger to them. They only knew her image on the screen, the same one I saw at the end of each day when I viewed the rushes with the rest of the company. "She" was Baby Peggy, who did what they saw up there, but I was the one responsible for how she did it, the difficult part, deserving of approval. These reactions were of course purely emotional, for I had no words to describe my feelings even to myself. But much of my uneasiness sprang from the curious first premise that I brought to my profession—that all adults had worked in movies as children. How else, indeed, had their parents survived? It came as a fresh surprise each time to discover that everyone, from my governess to the fan magazine writer, thought it a rare treat for a child to work in films.

Understandably, given the peculiar circumstances in which I found myself breadwinner for my family, I was intolerant of children who did not work. (That excepted my sister, Louise, for she sometimes worked as an extra in my comedies.) On those rare days when I stayed home and looked into the backyard of the elegant house next door and saw children playing in sandboxes and on swings, and screaming their way down the shining slides, I was filled with a sense of bewilderment that, as the years passed, turned into a feeling of unspeakable outrage. How could they? Where was their sense of responsibility to their families, their self-respect, their pride? Similarly, when children who worked with me on the set staged tantrums and insisted on being primed with ice cream before they would do a scene, I suffered from acute embarrassment, feeling that my peers had somehow betrayed me. For the lazy sandbox bums I harbored a degree of compassion because of their apparent ignorance of the way things should be. For the badly behaved studio child, however, I felt nothing but undisguised contempt.

I also picked up a protective attitude toward Mother; in fact, toward all women who did not work. Not only were they to be shielded from the labors and risks involved in our career (Father's and mine were one), they must also be protected from any unnecessary worry and preoccupation over the chances we were taking. Perhaps one reason my recollections of those early days are so vivid is that I was recording everything that was happening on two levels simultaneously: the action itself and the carefully edited version I would relate to Mother that night. Working mostly with men, I unconsciously absorbed the prevailing male attitude toward keeping "the lithe little woman" safe at home. Throughout the rest of my life, it would be difficult to relate to other women except on a professional basis, while with men I immediately assumed that a working relationship existed by the very fact that they were men.

I worked for the satisfaction of a job well done and for the respect and approval of Father and my coworkers. It was a wordless compensation, cutting across all barriers of sex and age, because making movies was serious business and, as no one at Century could forget, a very costly one. I reflected Father's own pride in performance and, possibly through my constant exposure to him and his cowboy friends who so often worked with me, I picked up their decisive way of dealing with challenging or dangerous situations.

While different directors were assigned to my comedies, it was Father who translated their demands to me. He based his logic on what he knew about horses, reasoning that a promising green colt could be ruined if handled by different riders, while a top cutting horse could result from one man's patient training. This gave him some small degree of control over my safety in what proved to be the very risky occupation of making slapstick comedies.

At Century (and later at Hal Roach, Educational, Mascot, and Monogram—wherever *Our Gang* and its imitators employed children), the perils sprang from carelessness of the safety factors. That, and a firm belief on the part of most adults with whom movie children worked that youngsters were physically indestructible, conspired to create potentially dangerous work situations.

Over the months I was made sick by having to work all day in a bathtub of sour whipped cream (to simulate soapsuds), I was nearly drowned in Santa Monica's ten-foot surf, and I was thrown from a speeding pickup truck together with the terrified goat to which I had been wired. A passenger train that was to be used as a prop in a railroad scene pulled out of the station minutes before Brownie and I were to work under the wheels. I was hit and dragged by a speeding bicycle, and my road burns were painted with white iodine, a cosmetic concession to my career but hardly a painless remedy. In every case, when the ordeal was behind me, I faced one almost as painful—how to keep from telling Mother the truth of what had happened at the studio that day.

Years later I found that my experience was about average for a movie child. Shirley Temple claimed that the things she was made to do while filming her Baby Burlesks were so dangerous that directors barred the mothers from the set. And Darla Hood of *Our Gang* recalls spending half a day hanging onto the back of a dogcatcher's wagon, shooting the same scene over and over again until she was finally overcome by carbon monoxide fumes and passed out cold.

FROM "UNDER THE HOLLYWOOD SIGN"

On the southwest corner of Hollywood Boulevard and Western Avenue, an office building housed an institution indispensable to the making of motion pictures, Central Casting. Right next door to it on Hollywood Boulevard, a second building housed an equally vital but less well-known establishment, Lawlor's Professional School. Here on the second floor, 150 harassed movie children, from toddlers to teenagers, struggled to get what passed for an education. Lawlor's was not yet accredited by the state, tuition was $25 a month, studying was everyone's spare-time activity, and the place looked like the prop department's idea of a school. But compared to the alternatives, it was seventh heaven.

About one-third of Lawlor's enrollment was composed of former child actors and stars like myself, all trying to navigate the treacherous reefs of adolescence toward a landfall of adult fame. Another third were as-yet-undiscovered children, snatching at every extra job and scrap of dialogue in an effort to pull themselves up to stardom. In my time nearly a dozen of these plucky youngsters made it: Mickey Rooney, Judy Garland, Jane Withers, Charlotte Henry, Betty Grable, Gower Champion, Juanita Quigley, Anne Shirley, Virginia Weidler, and Edith Fellows.

Sandwiched in between were some three score luckless juveniles destined to make it big only on the neighborhood beer-hall circuit. They danced and sang bawdy songs for $5 a night in "queer joints" such as the infamous B.B.B.'s Cellar and similar dives on Santa Monica Boulevard and lower Western Avenue. They came to school each morning half asleep and only began waking up at noon. They had never been famous, nor would they ever be. Worse still, they knew it. But they were the sole support of their families, and perhaps that is why the welfare authorities seemed to be willfully blind to their existence.

Lawlor's great virtue was that it offered Hollywood children a refuge where they would not be regarded as freaks by teachers and classmates. As a freshman at Fairfax High, I had been buried alive for six months in a class for severely retarded children simply because I had never learned algebra. Whenever Louise and I worked extra, we received a demerit from the office for being absent. Matching time had to be spent in a detention hall with other delinquents whose crimes ranged from smoking in the restrooms to acknowledged vandalism. When Judy Garland tried to enroll at Hollywood High, the vice principal informed her coldly, "Children like you should not be allowed to go to school with normal children!" Small wonder we all preferred serving our time at Lawlor's.

The education of movie children had always been a contradiction in terms. After all, any five-year-old who can earn $2,000 a week without being able to read and write does not appear to have a handicap, especially to his or her parents; obviously the child did not need an education. To most movie parents, school was simply an obstacle to be gotten around with the maximum speed and minimum time. Traditionally, parents and studio bosses conspired to sabotage the efforts of welfare workers and teachers on the set, whom they regarded as their natural enemies. The more time the children worked, the more money they earned and the sooner their career got off the ground; this was the parental position. Directors and producers likewise considered time spent on schooling as money thrown away—in addition to the teacher's salary, they were required by law to pay. In consequence, the four hours supposed to be set aside for children's schoolwork on the set were more often than not observed in the breach. So-called play or rest periods of some two hours daily were nearly always ignored and plowed back into production time. When we did study, we had to do so under almost impossible conditions, usually right on the set. Nevertheless, dedicated women such as Fern Carter, Mary McDonald, and a lady known only as Mrs. West were more than equal to the challenge.

Mrs. Carter was for years the regular teacher of the *Our Gang* members. She even accompanied Darla Hood, Spanky McFarland, and Buckwheat when they went on a personal appearance tour. To Mrs. Carter fell the unpleasant task of trying to explain to worried Darla why Buckwheat and his mother had to ride in a different Pullman car and stay in special hotels on the road. When Mrs. Carter finished with the white children's lessons, she made the long trek back to Buckwheat's car, where she instructed him in antiseptic isolation from the rest of his longtime friends.

Mary McDonald ran the Little Red Schoolhouse at MGM. Among her world-renowned students were Roddy McDowall, Margaret O'Brien, Elizabeth Taylor, Mickey Rooney, Judy Garland, and briefly Freddie Bartholomew, the English-born star of *David Copperfield* and *Little Lord Fauntleroy*. When the studio noticed that fraternization with the others was causing Freddie to lose his clipped British accent, a commodity every bit as priceless as his acting skills, he was pulled out of school and assigned a private tutor, Mrs. Murphy from Ireland. Thereafter, Freddie and his regular stand-in, Ray Sperry, studied together in a makeshift booth on the set. Even Ray emerged from these sessions speaking like a British lord.

Mrs. West taught at various studios, but at Paramount she won industrywide acclaim for having faced down the great Cecil B. DeMille himself.

"I didn't like the way you played that scene," DeMille told Dickie Moore one day after a take. The always proper and polite Dickie, who felt unusually tired and irritable, responded with an offhand, "Who cares?" Infuriated, DeMille raised his arm to strike the child when he suddenly found himself confronting Dickie's avenging angel, a wrathful Mrs. West. Planting her ample-bosomed figure squarely between Dickie and DeMille, she declared in tones that rang across the quiet set: "You lay one hand on that child and this picture doesn't move!" The best allies some children had were their fearless studio teachers.

The head of Lawlor's school was a woman cast in the same Amazonian mold. Viola F. Lawlor, or "Mom," as she insisted on being called, was a plain, large-boned Yankee from Concord, New Hampshire. Pure American Gothic on the outside, her innermost soul was committed to Hollywood, and movie children were her weakness. Her special favorites were Mickey Rooney and Frankie Darro, both boys from broken homes. Mickey was still doing bits under the aegis of Harry Weber. Frankie was a star, a veteran of the rough-and-tumble Mascot serials that costarred him with Rin Tin Tin and won him a special place in the hearts of Saturday matinee audiences everywhere.

Although the curriculum at Lawlor's was so informal as to be almost nonexistent, Mom liked to think of herself as a strict disciplinarian. "Don't think you're going to lord it over anybody here just because you were Baby Peggy!" was her frosty welcome to me. Whenever there was an uproar in the study hall, which was often, she could be seen striding purposefully down the long corridor, breathing fire and preparing thunderbolts. But if she discovered that it was Frankie dancing on the library table wrapped in a tablecloth, or Mickey standing on a desk doing an imitation of Lionel Barrymore or Clark Gable, she relaxed and signaled them to go on with the show. Folding her arms and smiling, she enjoyed the performance as much as if she had bought a ticket.

One day she confided to me that she spoiled Frankie because she felt so sorry for him. His mother, the former Italian aerialist who had never worked again after her nervous breakdown in Long Beach, now lived in the apartment house across the street from the school. Since the Darros were separated and Frankie lived with his father, the only way she could catch a glimpse of her famous son was at the movies or when he entered and left school. After that, I always watched for Mrs. Darro, and sure enough, every day as school let out the curtain would be drawn back from the window and for a brief moment her face would appear. To me it was the most poignant of scenes, made even more so by its setting against the backdrop of the slate gray Hollywood Hills. It represented only one among thousands of similar personal tragedies being played out under the uncaring gaze of the forever-tipsy Hollywood sign, whose increasingly grimy letters seemed about to fall off the scrubby mountainside.

School hours at Lawlor's only took up half a day—usually the least profitable ones at that, since interviews were rarely held in the early-morning hours. There were about ten rooms scattered around a main hall, and most of them were equipped with mirrors, practice bars, and pianos. By one o'clock the classrooms had been cleared for action, the desks and chairs pushed back against the walls. For the rest of the afternoon and evening, those who had been scholars turned into troupers, everyone practicing their juggling, tap routines, ballet, opera, blues singing, piano, violin, trumpet, diction, nip-ups, and contortions.

The shows put on twice a year by Lawlor students were a far cry from the average amateurish school production. Mickey or Frankie served as MC and stand-up comic, often aided by Sidney Miller, one of Mickey's lifelong sidekicks. Jane Withers glimmered through her tap numbers, and an incredibly innovative dancer, fourteen-year-old Gower Champion, fairly ricocheted off the walls in routines that he created and rehearsed with infinite patience every day after school. Edith Fellows sang the "Jewel Song" from *Faust* in a voice that was uncannily vibrant for an eleven-year-old child. And, of course, after the Gumm sisters enrolled, Mom Lawlor always put Judy in the star position on the bill.

On her first day at Lawlor's in early 1934, Judy was a quiet, plain little girl whose dresses were a trifle too long and obviously homemade. She looked too old for a child, but she did not yet have the body of a woman. Mom brought her into our study hall, introduced her, and then asked her if she would sing a number for us. Ethel Gumm settled herself on the bench, and Judy clambered onto the top of the old upright piano. When she crossed her legs, I noticed the limp, worn taffeta bows on her tap shoes. They reminded me of my own tap shoes, whose soles had several times worn through, and what they told me about her made me want to cry. I thought it was needlessly cruel of Mrs. Lawlor to put this obvious amateur through such an ordeal; after all, she knew we were an audience of hardened professionals, and this was a poor little kid from the godforsaken desert town of Lancaster.

But we had misjudged both Judy and Mom. After Ethel Gumm swept through the introductory bars of the popular "Blue Moon," an incredibly rich voice charged with a mature woman's emotional power was flooding the room: "Blue Moon / You saw me standing alone / Without a dream in my heart / Without a love of my own...."

When Judy finished, there were tears of pride in Mom's eyes, and every student in the room was applauding wildly and cheering the forlorn little newcomer. Even then Judy was a professional's professional. At our annual Lawlor shows, staged at the Wilshire Ebell Theater, we kept giving Judy encores that sometimes kept her singing until two o'clock in the morning. She seemed unable to say no to an audience.

When Lawlor kids got together in one another's cramped Depression-era apartments, our idea of a good time was doing what we did for a livelihood. Not even necking was preferred above our all-time-favorite pastime, staging impromptu blackouts and musical shows. Mickey and his shadow, Sidney Miller, shared the nicest apartment in the better part of Hollywood, and it alone was big enough to serve our purpose well. Mickey also knew a good many blackout skits from his father, Joe Yule, whom Mickey had found and brought to Hollywood once his own career was getting under way. When Yule was not working at MGM as an extra or bit player, he served as the star comic in a burlesque house on Main Street in Los Angeles.

After the blackouts came the song-and-dance numbers, usually put together on the spot. One reason we all worked so well together is that everyone understood and used the same nonlinear, purely visual language of movement we had been taught by Ernest Belcher, Ethel Meglin, or the Mosconi brothers. Dance routines were like scripts, composed of hundreds of variations on basic steps and the sequences that stitched them together. When Shirley, Jane, Mickey, or Judy went into rehearsal on a set with a dance director, they merely had to learn his script, composed in a common shorthand they had mastered long before they knew their alphabet. At a party, we could put together a chorus line in minutes with Mickey calling the shots: "Okay, start with a basic time step, then a soft shoe segue into the Charleston, a backward drag and a windmill...."

Sometimes the police were called in to break up these marathon parties; they were not wild, but they were loud. Innocent though these gatherings were, they gave us all a much-needed outlet for severely repressed emotions. They allowed us to play together in the only way we could conceive of recreation, as a reprise of our work. We had neither the time nor the taste for the football rallies and proms that occupied average teenagers. The fierce competition between us in the daily struggle for bread made our friendships precarious and vulnerable to the demands of our careers. Only when we staged our own shows could we be noncompetitive, completely free of the contentious and divisive spirit generated by parents and others on the set.

PHOTO BY DANNY MARTINEZ

In fiction and in nonfiction, Naomi Hirahara has given life and breath to portrayals of Japanese immigrants and Japanese Americans in communities in Los Angeles and beyond. Linking her mysteries, biographies, business histories, and other works, a fascinating and well-researched through-line emerges. Each work offers a picture, from a variety of perspectives, of moments in the century-long timeline of communities establishing themselves. With fidelity, each also documents the effort of immigrants and American-born people to create opportunities for productive work in the face of racist government-policy obstacles. Taking individual stories as entry points, Hirahara has often focused on specific work and occupations, writing about gardeners, doctors, farmers, business owners, and, in this piece for *Paperback L.A.*, about fishermen. Here she expands on a small point in a history she coauthored with Geraldine Knatz, *Terminal Island: The Lost Communities of Los Angeles Harbor*, and delves a bit more deeply into the mystery of a Shinto shrine that was built in Fish Harbor, a "company town" of fishermen and cannery workers.

GHOST TOWN 2
FISH HARBOR

SHINTO SHRINES AND SHIPWRECKS: TALES OF FISH HARBOR

NAOMI HIRAHARA

FIRST THERE WAS THE SMELL. FOR OUTSIDERS, ANYONE *not* from the Terminal Island community known as Fish Harbor, the smell was awful. It apparently wasn't only the fresh fish—mackerel, tuna, sardines brought over on the wet and slick decks of boats and large vessels—but also the processing of these daily catches in local canneries and fertilizer factories.

Lloyd Inui, a native of nearby Long Beach, visited Fish Harbor with his family in the 1930s. He looked around at the crowded wooden structures that at the time housed about 2,000 people in a five-square-block area. The cannery-owned housing was divided by streets named Tuna, Barracuda, and even Albicore (charmingly misspelled). Lloyd was only a child at the time, but he said it was immediately clear to him: "This is a ghetto."

For Yutaka Dave Nakagawa, raised in Fish Harbor, located just east of San Pedro, it was quite a different story. This was his paradise, "where a youngster can go swimming in the crystal-clear water inside the harbor," play samurai and pirates on rock piles, snag giant crabs, and roast tasty potatoes near blazing campfires. Another Terminal Islander, Charlie Hamasaki, also described it as an enchanted island, "one big, happy community [in which] people help each other." And the smell? "The air is not smog air. It's vitamin E," he explained.

Today, the only evidence of their childhood homes is some modern street signs with those vintage names, a few stuccoed-over façades that used to be grocery and dry goods stores, and a monument on Seaside Avenue that features a reproduction of a *torii*, or traditional Japanese gateway that marks the entrance of a Shinto shrine.

Few visitors would understand the significance of the torii being represented in the monument. There's no shrine on Terminal Island now. And there's no Fish Harbor. In Japan, a torii marks the entrance of a sacred space. This reproduction of the torii that once marked a Shinto shrine at 226 Terminal Way is a reminder of tradition honored and dangers faced, but it's also a link to a past destroyed and a community erased. It's also a window on intriguing historical research that's not yet complete.

THE LURE OF FISH

Terminal Island had its origins in two pieces of land—Rattlesnake Island and Deadman's Island—separated by a jetty. As colorful as their names were and as pleasant as the view was in the early 1900s for wealthy families who vacationed there in large homes, the city of L.A. could not let the land and silt stay as it was. There was money to be made. Los Angeles was becoming a major metropolis with a harbor that was too narrow and too shallow to be of any real commercial use. The Army Corps of Engineers dredged the basin and deposited the silt in front of the seaward side of what was now Terminal Island. The fishing industry moved in where tourism had moved out, attracting immigrant workers—fishermen from Japan, Italy, and Yugoslavia.

By 1917, several canneries had opened, along with housing for workers' families. Southern California Fish Company, International Packing Company, American Tuna Company, French Sardine Company, and White Star Canning Company were all lined up along Wharf Street in the new town of Fish Harbor, created by the city of Los Angeles on reclaimed land. South of Vincent Thomas Bridge, across the channel from and east of San Pedro, Fish Harbor had direct access to the ocean and, eventually, a quarter-mile main street of shops and businesses.

Even before the canneries, Issei (Japanese immigrant) fishermen originally from Wakayama, a seaside prefecture along Kii Channel, had abandoned their work on the Southern Pacific Railroad to again pick up bamboo rods and fish like they had learned back home. Fastening barbless hooks on their rods, they threw bait with their hands into the ocean in front of them, dipped their lines in the water, and, feeling the tension of a fish on a line, flicked their wrists back. Through this artful technique, a caught tuna would fly overhead and land behind them. Observers were amazed—and soon these Issei were manning more than a third of the tuna boats in the San Pedro region.

Fishermen from different lands had their own unique fishing methods. The Italians, for example, were known for their *lampara* boats, a step up from the *ken-ken*, or jig boats, that the solo Japanese fisherman lined with hooks to snag fish. While the jig boats were small, with only five- to ten-horsepower gas engines, the lampara could be forty-five feet long. Five to twelve crew members pulled in fish caught in nets fastened around a ring.

The Yugoslavians were the masters of large vessels, the purse seiners, which were rigged with large nets buoyed by strings of giant cork. The nets were placed around schools of fish and then cinched closed like the drawstrings of a purse, trapping the mackerel and sardines.

A few miles away from the cannery area of the island was the town of Terminal, a multiethnic community that was home to workers in a variety of industries. While the Italians and Yugoslavians had vibrant communities on the "mainland" of San Pedro, the Japanese fishermen and their families, for the most part, made their home in the cannery housing of Fish Harbor. For $6 a month, they lived in narrow wooden homes and shared a wood-burning bathhouse, or *furo*, with their neighbors. Most of the men fished, while the women worked along the conveyor belts in the canneries.

It was a physically challenging life, ruled by the tides. Every night, Mas Tanibata, his mother, and siblings assisted his father, the operator of a one-man ken-ken boat, in untangling and baiting at least five lines, each supporting 400 to 500 hooks. His mother, who usually worked eight to ten hours at the cannery, would work until the wee hours of the morning to complete this labor-intensive preparation. "Seeing how hard she worked, we couldn't just sit around idly or go out to play with the other kids," he said. "So my brother and I used to help her."

As soon as boats with fresh catches reached Fish Harbor, a siren distinctive to that particular cannery would ring out through the area. Soon, women wearing their aprons, white caps, and boots would appear in the dirt streets, ready to report to work. Neighbors watched over children and infants, or sometimes the babies were placed in open boxes at the cannery while their mothers packed cans with freshly steamed fish.

The recruitment of Japanese immigrants as laborers was all about commerce, but the funny thing is, when you push and pull people into new places, culture grows, sometimes in unexpected ways. Even the culture that was directed from above by municipal leaders took a slight detour.

Take religion. The Wakayama fishermen had allegiances to the Buddhist temple in Little Tokyo. Methodism was the popular denomination among Japanese American Christian converts, but because the Baptist church viewed Terminal Island as almost a foreign land, it decided to establish a mission there. The First Baptist Church of San Pedro dispatched a group of female parishioners to Terminal Island to instruct the Issei women in English and crocheting. In the 1920s, the Baptists built a church building within Fish Harbor and Nisei (American-born) children were recruited to attend Seisho Gakuen, Japanese-language "Bible School," after a full day of public school.

The Fish Harbor families were a bit torn. They didn't want to reject the offerings by these kind religious workers, nor did they want to abandon Buddhism. It was not uncommon for one child to attend the Baptist mission, while another child from the same family was sent to the Buddhist temple that was established in Fish Harbor in the 1930s. It was only diplomatic, families decided.

Another religion, Shinto, came on the Terminal Island scene in 1931. Shinto is a belief system unique to Japan and linked to a creation story related to the archipelago. At that time, most wedding ceremonies in Japan were Shinto, and the new year usually called for a visit to a Shinto shrine. However, in the United States, Shinto shrines were few and far between. Buddhism and its various sects had found root throughout Japanese American farm communities and major cities, but the presence of Shintoism was really only evident in Hawaii. That is, until San Pedro Daijin-Gu was established in Fish Harbor and became a landmark, now lost, of the Japanese on the island.

Marked by a torii gate constructed of wood and two fox statues, the shrine was located on Terminal Way in front of the judo hall. The shrine itself was a simple one-room structure with a traditional Japanese sloped roof. It can be known today only in photographs, and its origins remain mysterious.

According to the Japanese-language history book *San Pidoro Doho Hattenroku*, a man named Shinkichi Miyoshi spearheaded the idea to create a Shinto shrine at Fish Harbor. Born on October 1, 1878, in Hiroshima, Miyoshi didn't seem to follow the traditional path of a religious leader. He came to the United States through Hawaii, where he worked in the theater business. As a divorced father, he and his only child, Fumiko, settled on Terminal Island, where he worked in a restaurant.

Papers of Masaru Ben Akahori filed in UCLA Library's Special Collections provide more details. Akahori was a gifted entrepreneurial writer who ran a legal and advertising office on Terminal Island. Akahori submitted a lease permit for the shrine, then called the North American Shinto Temple, East San Pedro Branch, to the Harbor Commission. Once the permit was accepted in March 1931, restaurateur Shinkichi Miyoshi departed for Daijin-Gu shrine in Honolulu, Hawaii, for religious study. After two months, he returned to Terminal Island as a Shinto priest. In 1933, the shrine, now officially named the San Pedro Daijin-Gu, was formally registered as a nonprofit organization in California, with Miyoshi given the power of attorney.

Key to Shintoism is the enshrinement of the *kami*, or sacred spirit. Usually that kami needs to originate from another *jinja*, or shrine, and so the connection with the Honolulu Daijin-Gu was probably significant. But this enshrinement was also a bit nontraditional as well. In the June 8, 1935, issue of the *Straits Times*, a Singaporean newspaper, a brief article reported that photos of two American presidents, George Washington and Abraham Lincoln, had been enshrined in a Shinto branch in Los Angeles on May 10. Their respective birthdays had been added to the Shinto calendar as days of worship. A photo taken seven years later verifies this enshrinement. It shows Shinkichi Miyoshi cleaning the interior of the shrine, with large photos of both Washington and Lincoln visible on the altar.

BLESSINGS AND STRUGGLES

Services were not regularly held at the shrine, and in interviews when they were adults, the Nisei of Fish Harbor, who were just children before World War II, struggled to remember exactly what Miyoshi did all day. After all, the Baptists and the Buddhists were teaching Japanese as well as sponsoring activities like Boy Scouts. How was Miyoshi able to support himself? Or was he just maintaining the Shinto shrine as a side activity?

Then Lynn Yoshiko Hori remembered. One of four daughters of Isaburo and Kin Hori, she witnessed Miyoshi visiting the homes of fishermen who were about to depart on long expeditions. Whether they were Christian or Buddhist, many Fish Harbor homes had a *kamidama*, or altar, placed on a shelf high on a wall. These altars often displayed *shide*, zigzag-shaped paper streamers that are often used in ceremonies to provide blessings.

In Fish Harbor, going out to sea could mean never returning home again. Miyoshi's visits, which most likely were rewarded by monetary *orei*, or gifts of thanks, gave the fishermen and their families a sense of comfort. Lynn Hori recalled that her father had even donated an anchor to be placed in front of the shrine, further symbolizing that fishing sometimes required supernatural help from high places.

Fishing remains one of the most dangerous jobs in the United States, but the sea was not the only threat to the Terminal Island fishermen's livelihood. In 1919, erudite Kihei Nasu, secretary and spokesman of the Southern California Japanese Fishermen's Association, testified to the physical challenges of the job in a letter to a congressional committee: "The drudgery and squalor of a fisherman's life has not appealed greatly to the American citizen, and probably never will, hence the ranks must be recruited from our foreign population."

The House Committee of Immigration and Naturalization was grappling with the topic of the Japanese in California. This population was proving to be a problem, according to US Senator James Phelan of San Francisco. In addition to the phenomenon of the Japanese picture brides coming to America, xenophobic Phelan was worried that the Japanese had too much control of California farms as well as easy access to the sea. He claimed that fishing boats were smuggling stowaways and the Japanese government was doing nothing to stop it. He railed against Issei fishermen in Monterey, San Diego, and, of course, the San Pedro area.

Nasu, who lived on Terminal Island with his wife and five American born children (the youngest daughter born right there on the island), fought back. Ninety-nine percent of fishermen in California were foreign born, and of that number only one-third was Japanese. Why target the Japanese when there were plenty of other immigrants from Europe?

Fighting against racist rhetoric and policies was a nasty business. Nasu saw the writing on the wall and returned to Japan with his brood of children in the 1920s. The Issei fishermen remained and hired a new secretary of the Southern California Japanese Fishermen's Association, Hirosaburo Yokozeki, a graduate of Stanford University. They needed someone who was educated and completely bilingual to defend them. Each year, Yokozeki would have to go to Sacramento and advocate for the Japanese immigrants to prevent California lawmakers from denying them commercial fishing licenses—as Washington and Oregon had done.

Hardened by the constant battles with nature and politicians, the Terminal Islanders had tough exteriors. Puritanical Japanese Americans on the mainland considered the people of Tāminaru (as the locals called their home) to be uncouth. The fishermen were already known for their distinctive speech patterns, a mix of the Wakayama dialect and the result of living in a tight, insular community. Working on the sea had made the men's skin dark, and encountering life-threatening dangers on a daily basis led to the abandoning of niceties. Also, since liquor was a no-no on long expeditions, when the full moon appeared, providing the men a break from sardine fishing (which was dependent on the dark cover of night), they headed out to Little Tokyo's bars, further confirming the stereotype that all Terminal Islanders were a wild bunch.

But people of the land had no idea what could happen on the sea. Kisaye Nakasaki Sato remembered the worried knot of women, including her mother, as storms hit. Even one-man ken-ken boats, which never ventured out that far, were stuck for days in coves to wait out the bad weather. One fisherman never made it back; his body was never recovered. Decades later, his clothing was finally buried in a cemetery plot. The same family later experienced another death at sea, and the man's wife vowed to never again look at the ocean for the rest of her life.

A more publicized fateful journey involved the *Belle Isle*, a purse seiner under the leadership of Captain John Ivan Gabelich, a cofounder of the Jugoslav Club of San Pedro. The *Belle Isle* was last seen leaving Terminal Island in June 1934 for a forty-day fishing expedition at Galapagos Island. Two months later, it was reported missing, and the navy was contacted to look for the vessel in Central American waters—but to no avail. One of the twelve men on board was Terminal Islander Takeshi Morizawa, thirty-five.

Charlie Hamasaki, the one who sees Tāminaru as enchanted, also heard stories of the destructive power of the sea, such as when Harumatsu Yamasaki and his crew, coming home with a boatload of sardines on the *Cleopatra*, hit a reef on a foggy night in 1924. All were killed. When Kiyoo Yamashita, four other partners, and the owners of the Van Camp cannery pooled resources to build the *Columbus*, a 200-ton, 125-foot vessel, Terminal Islanders followed its trial run to Catalina Island in smaller boats, cheering and tooting horns. But that grand vessel lasted only three years. It sank in Baja California. In that case, however, the shipwrecked men were able to survive on ship's provisions and were spotted by another tuna clipper and saved.

Why in the world would these immigrant men continue in this dangerous occupation? First of all, the monetary rewards could be great. As an apprentice fisherman in 1941, Hamasaki made $500 his first month during the height of sardine season. In contrast, "the guys working on the land" made $15 a week. (Anti-alien land laws in California also prevented Japanese immigrants from buying new farm properties.) It was this gamble, as well as the hypnotic call of the sea and the vibrant island life, that held the fishing village together. And although the Terminal Islanders were squeezed into tight, ghetto-like quarters in Fish Harbor, they could rely on one another and some allies— their white employers and non-Japanese schoolteachers and missionaries.

Mildred Obarr Walizer started teaching at East San Pedro School when it was established by the L.A. Board of Education in 1917. Although she lived in San Pedro, she often slept on a cot in the school. She was promoted to principal and made it a priority to introduce the island children to the outside world, even after they had gone on to middle and high schools in San Pedro. She took girls on trips to Palm Springs, the San Bernardino Mountains, and as far as San Francisco and Yosemite. The elders on the island recognized Walizer's earnest devotion to these children and raised $4,000—a fortune at that time—to honor her with a trip to the small villages in Wakayama, Japan, where they were from. After Walizer tragically passed away in 1931 from cancer, the school was named for her.

Virginia Swanson, another charismatic figure, came to the island in the 1930s. As a high school student, she had been so moved by a Japanese doctor who spoke at her Baptist church in Minneapolis that she wrote a paper about the anti-Asian legislation plaguing the Japanese in California. Soon after, she accepted a mission assignment with the Baptist church on Terminal Island.

Swanson was there on the island when news spread about Japan's bombing of Pearl Harbor on that fateful day of December 7, 1941. Boats were not allowed back into the harbor. Churchgoers and other mainland visitors were detained at the ferry station. Soon certain Issei leaders were rounded up from their homes and virtually disappeared, as far as their families were concerned.

The weather was dark that week, and Swanson wrote, "The phone was dead, food was hard to get, lights were blacked out in the evening, and it rained torrents. Wednesday evening we had our prayer meeting in the dark."

It only got worse for the Terminal Islanders. Stores were shuttered, and Italian, German, and Japanese aliens were all barred from going out to sea "under any conditions." Then on February 2, 1942, all Japanese fishermen were arrested and taken to the federal penitentiary for questioning. In this unprecedented roundup, Charlie Hamasaki, who was born in Japan but really only knew America, was hauled in and eventually sent on a mystery train ride that ended at an alien detention center in Bismarck, North Dakota. It was his first time seeing snow.

Back at Terminal Island, Virginia Swanson went to authorities and made appeals for the Japanese fishermen to be released but was unsuccessful. Families were now cut off from their livelihoods, and the Baptist mission attempted to provide aid.

On February 25, 1942, armed soldiers came to the humble homes of Fish Harbor to announce an official military decree. Each resident had forty-eight hours to move from Terminal Island. This exclusion order was island-wide, affecting not only Fish Harbor but also the people of Terminal, a few miles to the east.

For the Japanese American households, this was merely the first in a series of moves. A month later, just when they had found temporary housing on the mainland, they had to leave the West Coast for landlocked camps. The ocean would not be theirs for a while.

WHAT REMAINS

Shortly after the exodus of the families, the wooden homes of Fish Harbor were bulldozed down. The Shinto shrine was dismantled, and who knows whether the torii, the fox statues, or the portraits of Washington and Lincoln were thrown out, destroyed, or hidden.

According to government documents, the Shinto priest, sixty-six-year-old Shinkichi Miyoshi, was sent along with other Terminal Island men to an alien detention camp in Santa Fe, New Mexico. After the war, Miyoshi seems to have bounced around the United States, eventually dying in DeWitt Army Hospital in Alexandria, Virginia, on June 21, 1965.

Financed by Terminal Islanders, who were resurrected as a community when they formed an official group in 1971, a sculpture incorporating the torii of San Pedro Daijin-Gu now stands as a monument on Seaside Avenue. The extended families of Fish Harbor still gather twice a year, but the parties and picnics are usually held in cities like San Pedro or Buena Park. A couple of buildings from the busy days of Tuna Street remain, their façades completely altered by stucco and new windows and doors.

In the area are dumpsters of trash, and when the wind whips through, you almost expect to see tumbleweeds blowing through the main drag. If you close your eyes at Wharf and Tuna streets, you can imagine the Model Ts parked on the side of the street and fishermen unloading their catch or going into chandlery stores to buy new line, while women in white caps and boots wearily return from a long day of cannery work and teenagers emerge from the sweetshop.

But you cannot fool yourself for long. It's because of the smell. There is no smell in Fish Harbor anymore.

A great egret near its Malibu nest. April 15, 2011. 1/2000 sec.

WILD
BIRDS
IN L.A.

HARTMUT
WALTER

NATURE NOTE 2

L.A. County's bird list surpasses 400 different species detected between Santa Catalina and the San Gabriel Mountains. Where there are trees and shrubs, where there is a bit of water, there are birds: ravens, hawks, and gulls circling playgrounds or cormorants, grebes, and pelicans at the beach. The avifauna of urban L.A. changes every few years. Lately, crows, collared doves, and Allen's hummingbirds are numerous, while scrub jays and robins are rare in many areas. And to the photographer's delight, the beautiful western bluebird is a frequent resident of parks and golf courses.

In Los Angeles, the photographer has the benefit of relatively tame birds so used to surfers and hikers that they allow a close approach. Seen up close, birds are so colorful, so lively and entertaining! A feeder near a window permits an encounter with juncos and hummingbirds. Use binoculars on your outdoor hike, and for an even greater pleasure, a good camera and a long lens for video and photography. Birds move fast, and a sharp image often requires a shutter speed of 1/1000 of a second or less.

At the Sepulveda Recreation Area in Encino, Lake Balboa fills with coots, ducks, gulls, and dozens of double-crested cormorants feasting on the fish. The wildlife area hosts large American white pelicans that breed in Utah and winter here, along with visiting ospreys and turkey vultures. In Marina del Rey, gulls, brown pelicans, and elegant snowy egrets populate the pier and docks, hoping for handouts from fishermen. Residential areas are home to noisy parrot and parakeet species that feast on the leaves, flowers, and fruits of ornamental trees. Every few square miles of houses have a breeding pair of fierce red-tailed hawks, which anchor their nests in large trees and feed rats and pigeons to their chicks.

One of my favorite birding areas is Malibu Lagoon, a habitat for coots, ducks, shorebirds, and ospreys. Nearby, a large tree in the Malibu Country Mart parking lot is used by a small colony of beautiful egrets and herons—an extreme case of wild-bird coexistence with urban development. While you sip your cappuccino below the tree canopy, birds feed their chicks fish from the lagoon. As many as four species of the heron family breed in this single tree every year.

—H.W.

Brown pelicans resting at Malibu Lagoon. March 7, 2009. 1/400 sec.

Brown pelicans plunging into Santa Monica Bay. October 20, 2014. 1/1600 sec.

Great egret nestlings vying for space on their nest. Malibu Country Mart, May 26, 2015. 1/500 sec.

Egrets at their nesting colony in Malibu. July 19, 2011. 1/1250 sec.

A pair of white-tailed kites at Malibu's Legacy Park. September 6, 2013. 1/1600 sec.

A great blue heron flying at Malibu Lagoon. June 2, 2015. 1/1000 sec.

A male red-winged blackbird displaying at Malibu's Legacy Park. June 6, 2013. 1/1000 sec.

A great egret with a captured mouse. Malibu Lagoon, October 8, 2016. 1/1600 sec.

A northern mockingbird harasses a resident red-tailed hawk. Palms, June 28, 2017. 1/1000 sec.

Two nanday parakeets socializing in Solstice Canyon. January 3, 2017. 1/500 sec.

A male western bluebird at Veterans Park, West Los Angeles. December 30, 2012. 1/1600 sec.

A large assembly of California gulls wintering at Malibu Lagoon. December 17, 2011. 1/2000 sec.

Green heron clearing its throat, Lake Balboa, Van Nuys. October 14, 2016.

"Los Angeles hurt me racially…much more than any city I remember from the South," said Chester Himes in his autobiography. "It was the look on people's faces when you asked them about a job…They looked so goddamned startled that I even asked." That lofty bias became confrontive racism and federally implemented segregation in World War II Los Angeles. "Lunching at the Ritzmore," published in *The Crisis* magazine in 1942, was inspired by a time when Floyd Covington, the head of L.A.'s Urban League branch, was denied service at the Biltmore Hotel in downtown L.A. It's an example of the fiercely satiric work that is part of Himes's literary legacy as a member, with peers James Baldwin and Richard Wright, of what has been called "the Indignant Generation" of leftist African American writers who were active between the Harlem Renaissance and the Civil Rights eras. This story's three main characters are a white student, a white "drifter," and "a Negro at the edge of the group."

SIDEWALK DEBATE
A CASE STUDY

LUNCHING AT THE RITZMORE

CHESTER HIMES

IF YOU HAVE EVER BEEN TO THE BEAUTIFUL CITY OF LOS ANGELES, you will know that Pershing Square, a palm-shaded spot in the center of downtown, is the mecca of the motley. Here, a short walk up from "Skid Row," on the green-painted benches flanking the crisscrossed sidewalks, is haven for men of all races, all creeds, all nationalities, and of all stages of deterioration—drifters and hopheads and TBs and beggars and bums and bindle-stiffs and big sisters, clipped and clippers, fraternizing with the tired business men from nearby offices, with students from various universities, with the strutting Filipinos, the sharp-cat Mexican youths in their ultra drapes, with the colored guys from out South Central way.

It is here the old men come to meditate in the warm midday sun and watch the hustle and bustle of the passing younger world; here the job seekers with packed bags wait to be singled out for work; here the hunters relax, and the hunted keep vigil. It is here you will find your man, for a game of pool, for a game of murder.

Along the Hill Street side buses going west line up one behind the other to take you out to Wilshire, to Beverly Hills, to Hollywood, to Santa Monica, to Westwood, to the Valley; and the red cars and the yellow cars fill the street with clatter and clang. On the Fifth Street side a pale pink skyscraper overlooks a lesser structure of aquamarine, southern California architecture on the pastel side; and along Sixth Street there are various shops and perhaps an office building which you would not notice unless you had business there.

But you would notice the Ritzmore, swankiest of West Coast hotels, standing in solid distinction along the Olive Street side, particularly if you were hungry in Pershing Square. You would watch footmen opening doors of limousines and doormen escorting patrons underneath the marquee across the width of sidewalk to the brass and mahogany doorway, and you would see hands of other doormen extended from within to hold wide the glass doors so that the patrons could make an unhampered entrance. And after that, if your views leaned a little to the Left, which they likely would if you were hungry in Pershing Square, you would spit on the sidewalk and resume your discussion, your boisterous and heated and surprisingly often very well-versed discussion, on defense, or on the army, or the navy, or that "rat" Hitler, or "them Japs," or the FBI, or the "so and so" owners of Lockheed, or that (unprintable) Aimee Semple McPherson; on history and geography, on life and death; and you would just ignore the "fat sonsaguns" who entered the Ritzmore.

On this particular day, a discussion which had begun on the Soviet Union had developed into an argument on discrimination against Negroes, and a young University of Southern California student from Vermont stated flatly that he did not believe Negroes were discriminated against at all.

"If you would draw your conclusions from investigation instead of from agitation, you would find that most of the discrimination against Negroes exists only in communistic literature distributed by the Communist Party for organizational purposes," he went on. "As a matter of plain and simple fact, I have yet to visit a place where Negroes could not go. In fact, I think I've seen Negroes in every place I've ever been—hotels, theatres, concerts, operas...."

"Yass, and I bet they were working there, too," another young fellow, a drifter from Chicago, argued. "Listen, boy, I'm telling you, and I'm telling you straight, Negroes are out in this country. They can't get no work and they can't go nowhere, and that's a dirty shame for there're a lot of good Negroes, a lot of Negroes just as good as you and me."

Surveying the drifter from head to foot, his unshaven face, his shabby unpressed suit, his run-over, unpolished shoes, the student replied, "Frankly, that wouldn't make them any super race."

"Huh?"

"However, that is beside the point," the student continued, smiling. "The point is that most of what you term discrimination is simply a matter of taste, of personal likes and dislikes. For instance, if I don't like you, should I have to put up with your presence? No, why should I? But this agitation about Negroes being discriminated against by the Army and Navy and defense industries and being refused service by hotels and restaurants is just so much bosh."

"Are you kidding me, fellow?" the drifter asked suspiciously, giving the student a sharp look, "or are you just plain dumb? Say, listen—" and then he spied a Negro at the edge of the group. "Say, here's a colored fellow now; I suppose he knows whether he's being discriminated against or not."

"Not necessarily," the student murmured.

Ignoring him, the drifter called, "Hey, mister, you mind settling a little argument for us."

The Negro, a young brown-skinned fellow of medium build with regular features and a small mustache, pushed to the center of the group. He wore a pair of corduroy trousers and a slip-over sweater with a sport shirt underneath. "Say, mister, I been tryna tell this schoolboy—" the drifter began, but the Negro interrupted him, "I know, I heard you."

Turning to the student, he said, "I don't know whether you're kidding or not, fellow, but it ain't no kidding matter with me. Here I am, a mechanic, a good mechanic, and they're supposed to be needing mechanics everywhere. But can I get a job—no! I gotta stand down here and listen to guys like you make a joke out of it while the government is crying for mechanics in defense."

"I'm not making a joke out of it," the student stated. "If what you say is true, I'm truly sorry, mister; it's just hard for me to believe it."

"Listen, schoolboy," the drifter said, "I'll tell you what I'll do with you; I'll just bet you a dollar this boy—this man—can't eat in any of these restaurants downtown. I'll just bet you a dollar."

Now that a bet had been offered, the ten or twelve fellows crowded about who had remained silent out of respect for the Negro's feelings, egged it on, "All right, schoolboy, put up or shut up!"

"Well, if it's all right with you, mister," the student addressed the Negro, "I'll just take this young man up on that bet. But how are we going to determine?"

They went into a huddle and after a moment decided to let the Negro enter any restaurant of his choice, and if he should be refused service the student would pay off the bet and treat the three of them to dinners on

Central Avenue; but should he be served, the check would be on the drifter.

So the three of them, the student, the Negro, and the drifter, started down Hill Street in search of a restaurant. The ten or twelve others of the original group fell in behind, and shortly fellows in other groups about the square looked up and saw the procession, and thinking someone was giving away something somewhere, hurried to get in line. Before they had progressed half the length of the block, more than a hundred of the raggedy bums of Pershing Square were following them.

The pedestrians stopped to see what the commotion was all about, adding to the congestion; and then the motorists noticed and slowed their cars. Soon almost a thousand people had congregated on the sidewalk and a jam of alarming proportions had halted traffic for several blocks. In time the policeman at the corner of Sixth and Hill awakened, and becoming aware of the mob, rushed forth to investigate. When he saw the long procession from the square, he charged the three in front who seemed to be the leaders and shouted. "Starting a riot, eh! Communist rally, eh! Where do you think you're going?"

"We're going to lunch," the student replied congenially.

For an instant the policeman was startled out of his wits. "Lunch?" His face went slack and his mouth hung open. Then he got himself under control. "Lunch! What is this? I suppose all of you are going to lunch," he added sarcastically.

The student looked about at the crowd, then looked back. "I don't know," he confessed. "I'm only speaking for the three of us."

Shoving back among the others, the policeman snarled, "Now don't tell me that you're going to lunch, too?"

A big, raw-boned fellow in overalls spat a stream of tobacco juice on the grass, and replied, "That's right."

Red-faced and inarticulate, the policeman took off his hat and scratched his head. Never in the six years since he had been directing traffic at Sixth and Hill had he seen anyone leave Pershing Square for lunch. In fact, it had never occurred to him that they ate lunch. It sounded incredible. He wanted to do something. He felt that it was his duty to do something. But what? He was in a dilemma. He could not hinder them from going to lunch, if indeed they were going to lunch. Nor could he order them to move on, as they were already moving on. There was nothing for him to do but follow. So he fell in and followed.

The Negro, however, could not make up his mind. On Sixth Street, midway between Hill and Olive, he came to a halt. "Listen," he pointed out, "these guys are used to seeing colored people down here. All the domestic workers who work out in Hollywood and Beverly and all out there get off the U car and come down here and catch their buses. It ain't like if it was somewhere on the West Side where they ain't used to seeing them."

"What has that got to do with it?" the student asked.

"Naw, what I mean is this," he explained. "They're liable to serve me around here. And then you're going to think it's like that all over the city. And I know it ain't." Pausing for an instant, he added another point, "And besides, if I walk in there with you two guys, they're liable to serve me anyway. For all they know you guys might be some rich guys and I might be working for you; and if they refuse to serve me they might get in dutch with you. It ain't like some place in Hollywood where they wouldn't care."

When they had stopped, the procession behind them which by then reached around the corner down Hill Street had also stopped. This was the chance for which the policeman had been waiting. "Move on!" he shouted. "Don't block the sidewalk! What d'ya think this is?"

They all returned to the square and took up the argument where they had dropped it. Only now, it was just one big mob in the center of the square, waiting for the Negro to make up his mind.

"You see, he doesn't want to do it," the student was pointing out. "That proves my point. They won't go into these places, but yet they say they're being discriminated against."

Suddenly, the drifter was inspired. "All right, I'll tell you, let's go to the Ritzmore."

A hundred startled glances leveled on him, then lifted to the face of the brick and granite edifice across the street which seemed impregnated in rocklike respectability. The very audacity of the suggestion appealed to them. "That's the place, let's go there," they chimed.

"That's nonsense," the student snapped angrily. "He can't eat at the Ritzmore; he's not dressed correctly."

"Can you eat there?" the Negro challenged. "I mean just as you're dressed."

The student was also clad in a sweater and trousers, although his were of a better quality and in better condition than the Negro's. For a moment he considered the question, then replied, "To be fair, I don't know whether they would serve me or not. They might in the grill—"

"In the main dining room?" the drifter pressed.

Shaking his head, the student stated, "I really don't know, but if they will serve any of us they will serve him."

"Come on," the drifter barked, taking the Negro by the arm, and they set forth for the Ritzmore, followed by every man in Pershing Square—the bindle-stiffs and the beggars and the bums and the big sisters, the clipped and the clippers, the old men who liked to sit in the midday sun and meditate.

Seeing them on the move again, the policeman hastened from his post to follow.

They crossed Olive Street, a ragged procession of gaunt, unshaven, unwashed humanity, led by two young white men and one young Negro, passed the two doormen, who, seeing the policeman among them, thought they were all being taken to the clink. They approached the brass and mahogany doorway unchallenged, pushed open the glass doors, and entered the classical splendor of the Ritzmore's main lounge.

Imagine the consternation among the well-bred, superbly clad, highly heeled patrons; imagine the indignity of the room clerk as he pounded on his bell and yelled frantically, "Front! Front! Front!" Had the furniture been animate, it would have fled in terror; and the fine Oriental rugs would have been humiliated unendurably.

Outraged, the house officer rushed to halt this smelly mob, but seeing among them the policeman, who by now had lost all capacity for speech, stood with his mouth gaped open, wondering if perhaps it wasn't just the effects of that last brandy he had enjoyed in "217," after all. Stupidly, he reached out his hand to touch them to make certain they were real.

But before he could get his reflexes together, those in front had strolled past him and entered the main dining room, while, what seemed to him like thousands of others, pushed in from the street.

The student and the Negro and the drifter, along with ten or twelve others, took seats at three vacant tables. In unison the diners turned one horrified stare in their direction, and arose in posthaste only to be locked at the doorway by a shoving mass of men, struggling for a ringside view.

From all over the dining room the waiters ran stumbling toward the rear, and went into a quick, alarmed huddle, turning every now and then to stare at the group and then going into another huddle. The head waiter rushed from the kitchen and joined the huddle; and then the maître d'hôtel appeared and took his place. One by one the cooks, the first cook and the second cook and the third cook and the fourth cook on down to what seemed like the twenty-fourth cook (although some of them must have been dishwashers), stuck their heads through the pantry doorway and stared for a moment and then retired.

Finally, two waiters timidly advanced toward the tables and took their orders. Menus were passed about. "You order first," the student said to the Negro. However, as the menus were composed mostly of French words, the Negro could not identify anything but apple pie. So he ordered apple pie.

"I'll take apple pie, too," the student said; and the drifter muttered, "Make mine the same."

Everyone ordered apple pie.

One of the fellows standing in the doorway called back to those in the lobby who could not see.

"They served him."

"Did they serve him?"

"Yeah, they served him."

"What did they serve him?"

"Apple pie."

And it was thus proved by the gentlemen of Pershing Square that no discrimination exists in the beautiful city of Los Angeles. However, it so happened that the drifter was without funds, and the student found himself in the peculiar situation of having to pay off a bet which he had won.

This is a weird one. By dedicating his 1985 novel, *Death Is a Lonely Business*, to a Mount Rushmore of noir masters (Hammett, Chandler, Cain, and MacDonald), Ray Bradbury signaled that he was planting a flag in their territory. But what kind of flag? Homage? Spoof? Sincere effort? Viewed with skepticism by some critics and with bestseller-fan fawning by others, *Death* was Bradbury's first novel after a thirty-five-year gap. Today it works best when read as a fever-dream memoir of the young writer Bradbury was in the late 1940s, living on the cheap in a backwater neighborhood and writing what are now considered fantasy-classic short stories for the pulps. And as Venice writhes in the throes of transformative gentrification, Bradbury's overwrought depiction of the community as a fog-bound final home to a cast of cute-tragic seniors still has a sturdy underpinning of authenticity. Giant oil well pumps, a defunct roller-coaster, neighborhood canals, run-down "Moorish fortress" mansions, end-of-the-line trolleys—all were part of the scene.

GHOST TOWN 3
VENICE

DEATH IS A LONELY BUSINESS

RAY BRADBURY

VENICE, CALIFORNIA, IN THE OLD DAYS HAD MUCH TO recommend it to people who liked to be sad. It had fog almost every night and along the shore the moaning of the oil well machinery and the slap of dark water in the canals and the hiss of sand against the windows of your house when the wind came up and sang among the open places and along the empty walks.

Those were the days when the Venice pier was falling apart and dying in the sea and you could find there the bones of a vast dinosaur, the roller-coaster, being covered by the shifting tides.

At the end of one long canal you could find old circus wagons that had been rolled and dumped, and in the cages, at midnight, if you looked, things lived—fish and crayfish moving with the tide; and it was all the circuses of time somehow gone to doom and rusting away.

And there was a loud avalanche of big red trolley car that rushed toward the sea every half-hour and at midnight skirled the curve and threw sparks on the high wires and rolled away with a moan which was like the dead turning in their sleep, as if the trolleys and the lonely men who swayed steering them knew that in another year they would be gone, the tracks covered with con-crete and tar and the high spider-wire collected on rolls and spirited away.

And it was in that time, in one of those lonely years when the fogs never ended and the winds never stopped their laments, that riding the old red trolley, the high-bucketing thunder, one night I met up with Death's friend and didn't know it.

It was a raining night, with me reading a book in the back of the old, whining, roaring railcar on its way from one empty confetti-tossed transfer station to the next. Just me and the big, aching wooden car and the conductor up front slamming the brass controls and easing the brakes and letting out the hell-steam when needed.

And the man down the aisle who somehow had got there without my noticing.

I became aware of him finally because of him swaying swaying, standing there behind me for a long time, as if undecided because there were forty empty seats and late at night it is hard with so much emptiness to decide which one to take. But finally I heard him sit and I knew he was there because I could smell him like the tidelands coming in across the fields. On top of the smell of his clothes, there was the odor of too much drink taken in too little time.

I did not look back at him. I learned long ago, looking only encourages. I shut my eyes and kept my head firmly turned away. It didn't work.

"Oh," the man moaned.

I could feel him strain forward in his seat. I felt his hot breath on my neck. I held on to my knees and sank away.

"Oh," he moaned, even louder. It was like someone falling off a cliff, asking to be saved, or someone swimming far out in the storm, wanting to be seen.

"Ah!"

It was raining hard now as the big red trolley bucketed across a midnight stretch of meadow-grass and the rain banged the windows, drenching away the sight of open fields. We sailed through Culver City without seeing the film studio and ran on, the great car heaving, the floorboard whining under-foot, the empty seats creaking, the train whistle screaming.

And a blast of terrible air from behind me as the unseen man cried, "Death!"

The train whistle cut across his voice so he had to start over.

"Death—"

Another whistle.

"Death," said the voice behind me, "is a lonely business."

I thought he might weep. I stared ahead at the flashing rain that rushed to meet us. The train slowed. The man rose up in a fury of demand, as if he might beat at me if I didn't listen and at last turn. He wanted to be seen. He wished to drown me in his need. I felt his hands stretch out, and whether as fists or claws, to rake or beat me, I could not guess. I clutched the seat in front of me. His voice exploded.

"Oh, death!"

The train braked to a halt.

Go on, I thought, finish it!

"Is a lonely business!" he said, in a dreadful whisper, and moved away.

I heard the back door open. At last I turned.

The car was empty. The man had gone, taking his funeral with him. I heard gravel crunching on the path outside the train.

The unseen man was muttering out there to himself as the doors banged shut. I could still hear him through the window. Something about the grave. Something about the grave. Something about the lonely.

The train jerked and roared away through the long grass and the storm.

I threw the window up to lean out and stare back into wet darkness.

If there was a city back there, and people, or one man and his terrible sadness, I could not see, nor hear.

The train was headed for the ocean.

I had this awful feeling it would plunge in.

I slammed the window down and sat, shivering.

I had to remind myself all the rest of the way, you're only twenty-seven. You don't drink. But....

I had a drink, anyway.

Here at this far lost end of the continent, where the trail wagons had stopped and the people with them, I found a last-stand saloon, empty save for a bartender in love with Hopalong Cassidy on late night TV.

"One double vodka, please."

I was astounded at my voice. Why was I drinking? For courage to call my girlfriend, Peg, two thousand miles away in Mexico City? To tell her that I was all right? But nothing had happened to me, had it?

Nothing but a train ride and cold rain and a dreadful voice behind me, exhaling vapors of fear. But I dreaded going back to my apartment bed, which was as empty as an icebox abandoned by the Okies on the way west.

The only thing emptier was my Great American Novelist's bank account in an old Roman temple bank building on the edge of the sea, about to be washed away in the next recession. The tellers waited in rowboats every morning, while the manager drowned himself in the nearest bar. I rarely saw any of them. With only an occasional sale to a pulp detective magazine, there was no cash to deposit. So....

I drank my vodka. I winced.

"Jesus," said the bartender, "you look like you never had booze before!"

"I never did."

"You look horrible."

"I feel horrible. You ever think something awful is going to happen, but you don't know what?"

"It's called the heebie-jeebies."

I swallowed more vodka and shivered.

"No, no. Something really terrible, closing in on you, is what I mean."

The bartender looked over my shoulder as if he saw the ghost of the man on the train there.

"Did you bring it in with you?"

"No."

"Then it's not here."

"But," I said, "he spoke to me—one of the Furies."

"Furies?"

"I didn't see his face. God, I feel worse now. Good night."

"Lay off the booze!"

But I was out the door and peering in all directions to catch the thing that was waiting for me. Which way home, so as not to meet up with darkness? I chose.

And knowing it was the wrong choice, I hurried along the dark rim of the old canal toward the drowned circus wagons.

How the lion cages got in the canal no one knew. For that matter, no one seemed to remember how the canals had gotten there in the middle of an old town somehow fallen to seed, the seeds rustling against the doors every night along with the sand and bits of seaweed and unravelings of tobacco from cigarettes tossed along the strand-shore as far back as 1910.

But there they were, the canals and, at the end of one, a dark green- and oil-scummed waterway, the ancient circus wagons and cages, flaking their white enamel and gold paint and rusting their thick bars.

A long time before, in the early Twenties, these cages had probably rolled by like bright summer storms with animals prowling them, lions opening their mouths to exhale hot meat breaths. Teams of white horses had dragged their pomp through Venice and across the fields long before MGM put up its false fronts and made a new kind of circus that would live forever on bits of film.

Now all that remained of the old parade had ended here. Some of the cage wagons stood upright in the deep waters of the canal, others were tilted flat over on their sides and buried in the tides that revealed them some dawns or covered them some midnights. Fish swarmed in and out of the bars. By day small boys came and danced about on the huge lost islands of steel and wood and sometimes popped inside and shook the bars and roared.

But now, long after midnight with the last trolley gone to destinations north along the empty sands, the canals lapped their black waters and sucked at the cages like old women sucking their empty gums.

I came running, head down against the rain which suddenly cleared and stopped. The moon broke through a rift of darkness like a great eye watching me. I walked on mirrors which showed me the same moon and clouds. I walked on the sky beneath, and—something happened....

From somewhere a block or so away, a tidal surge of salt water came rolling black and smooth between the canal banks. Somewhere a sandbar had broken and let the sea in. And here the dark waters came. The tide reached a small overpass bridge at the same moment I reached the center.

The water hissed about the old lion cages.

I quickened. I seized the rail of the bridge.

For in one cage, directly below me, a dim phosphorescence bumped the inside of the bars.

A hand gestured from within the cage.

Some old lion-tamer, gone to sleep, had just wakened to find himself in a strange place.

An arm outstretched within the cage, behind the bars, languidly. The lion-tamer was coming full awake.

The water fell and rose again.

And a ghost pressed to the bars.

Bent over the rail, I could not believe.

But now the spirit-light took shape. Not only a hand, an arm, but an entire body sagged and loosely gesticulated, like an immense marionette, trapped in iron.

A pale face, with empty eyes which took light from the moon, and showed nothing else, was there like a silver mask.

Then the tide shrugged and sank. The body vanished.

Somewhere inside my head, the vast trolley rounded a curve of rusted track, chocked brakes, threw sparks, screamed to a halt as somewhere an unseen man jolted out those words with every run, jump, rush.

"Death—is a lonely—business."

No.

The tide rose again in a gesture like a stance remembered from some other night.

And the ghost shape rose again within the cage.

It was a dead man wanting out.

Somebody gave a terrible yell.

I knew it was me when a dozen lights flashed on in the little houses along the rim of the dark canal.

"All right, stand back, stand back!"

More cars were arriving, more police, more lights going on, more people wandering out in their bathrobes, stunned with sleep, to stand with me, stunned with more than sleep. We looked like a mob of miserable clowns abandoned on the bridge, looking down at our drowned circus.

I stood shivering, staring at the cage, thinking, why didn't I look back? Why didn't I see that man who knew all about the man down there in the circus wagon?

My God, I thought, what if the man on the train had actually shoved this dead man into the cage!

Proof? None. All I had was five words repeated on a night train an hour after midnight. All I had was rain dripping on the high wire repeating those words. All I had was the way the cold water came like death along the canal to wash the cages and go back out colder than when it had arrived.

More strange clowns came out of the old bungalows.

"All right, folks, it's three in the morning. Clear away!"

It had begun to rain again, and the police when they had arrived had looked at me as if to say, why didn't you mind your own business? or wait until morning and phone it in, anonymous?

One of the policemen stood on the edge of the canal in a pair of black swim trunks, looking at the water with distaste. His body was white from not having been in the sun for a long while. He stood watching the tide move into the cage and lift the sleeper there, beckoning. A face showed behind the bars.

The face was so gone-far-off-away it was sad. There was a terrible wrenching in my chest. I had to back off, because I heard the first trembling cough of grief start up in my throat.

And then the white flesh of the policeman cut the water. He sank.

I thought he had drowned, too. The rain fell on the oily surface of the canal.

And then the officer appeared, inside the cage, his face to the bars, gagging.

It shocked me, for I thought it was the dead man come there for a last in-sucked gasp of life.

A moment later, I saw the swimmer thrashing out of the far side of the cage, pulling a long ghost shape like a funeral streamer of pale seaweed. Someone was mourning. Dear Jesus, it can't be me!

They had the body out on the canal bank now, and the swimmer was toweling himself. The lights were blinking off in the patrol cars. Three policemen bent over the body with flashlights, talking in low voices.

"—I'd say about twenty-four hours."

"—Where's the coroner?"

"—Phone's off the hook. Tom went to get him."

"Any wallet—I.D.?"

"He's clean. Probably a transient."

They started turning the pockets inside out.

"No, not a transient," I said, and stopped.

One of the policemen had turned to flash his light in my face. With great curiosity he examined my eyes, and heard the sounds buried in my throat.

"You know him?"

"No."

"Then why—?"

"Why am I feeling lousy? Because. He's dead, forever. Christ. And I found him."

My mind jumped.

On a brighter summer day years back I had rounded a corner to find a man sprawled under a braked car. The driver was leaping from the car to stand over the body. I stepped forward, then stopped.

Something pink lay on the sidewalk near my shoe.

I remembered it from some high school laboratory vat. A lonely bit of brain tissue.

A woman, passing, a stranger, stood for a long time staring at the body under the car. Then she did an impulsive thing she could not have anticipated. She bent slowly to kneel by the body. She patted his shoulder, touched him gently as if to say, oh there, there, there, oh, oh—there.

"Was he—killed?" I heard myself say.

The policeman turned. "What made you say that?"

"How would, I mean, how would he get in that cage—underwater—if someone didn't—stuff him there?"

The flashlight switched on again and touched over my face like a doctor's hand, probing for symptoms.

"You the one who phoned the call in?"

"No." I shivered. "I'm the one who yelled and made all the lights come on."

"Hey," someone whispered.

A plainclothes detective, short, balding, kneeled by the body and turned out the coat pockets. From them tumbled wads and clots of what looked like wet snowflakes, papier-mâché.

"What in hell's that?" someone said.

I know, I thought, but didn't say.

My hand trembling, I bent near the detective to pick up some of the wet paper mash. He was busy emptying the other pockets of more of the junk. I kept some of it in my palm and, as I rose, shoved it in my pocket, as the detective glanced up.

"You're soaked," he said. "Give your name and address to that officer over there and get home. Dry off."

It was beginning to rain again and I was shivering. I turned, gave the officer my name and address, and hurried away toward my apartment.

I had jogged along for about a block when a car pulled up and the door swung open. The short detective with the balding head blinked out at me.

"Christ, you look awful," he said.

"Someone else said that to me, just an hour ago."

"Get in."

"I only live another block—"

"Get in!"

I climbed in, shuddering, and he drove me the last two blocks to my thirty-dollar-a-month, stale, crackerbox flat. I almost fell, getting out, I was so weak with trembling.

"Crumley," said the detective. "Elmo Crumley. Call me when you figure out what that paper junk is you stuck in your pocket."

I started guiltily. My hand went to that pocket. I nodded. "Sure."

"And stop worrying and looking sick," said Crumley. "He wasn't any-body—." He stopped, ashamed of what he had said, and ducked his head to start over.

"Why do I think he was somebody?" I said. "When I remember who, I'll call."

I stood frozen. I was afraid more terrible things were waiting just behind me. When I opened my apartment door, would black canal waters flood out?

"Jump!" and Elmo Crumley slammed his door.

His car was just two dots of red light going away in a fresh downpour that beat my eyelids shut.

I glanced across the street at the gas station phone booth which I used as my office to call editors who never phoned back. I rummaged my pockets for change, thinking, I'll call Mexico City, wake Peg, reverse the charges, tell her about the cage, the man, and—Christ—scare her to death!

Listen to the detective, I thought.

Jump.

I was shaking so violently now that I couldn't get the damn key in the lock.

Rain followed me inside.

Inside, waiting for me was….

An empty twenty-by-twenty studio apartment with a body-damaged sofa, a bookcase with fourteen books in it and lots of waiting space, an easy chair bought on the cheap from Goodwill Industries, a Sears, Roebuck unpainted pinewood desk with an unoiled 1934 Underwood Standard typewriter on it, as big as a player piano and as loud as wooden clogs on a carpetless floor.

In the typewriter was an anticipatory sheet of paper. In a wood box on one side was my collected literary output, all in one stack. There were copies of *Dime Detective*, *Detective Tales*, and *Black Mask*, each of which had paid me thirty or forty dollars per story. On the other side was another wooden box, waiting to be filled with manuscript. In it was a single page of a book that refused to begin.

UNTITLED NOVEL.

With my name under that. And the date, July 1, 1949.

Which was three months ago.

I shivered, stripped down, toweled myself off, got into a bathrobe, and came back to stand staring at my desk.

I touched the typewriter, wondering if it was a lost friend or a man or a mean mistress.

Somewhere back a few weeks it had made noises vaguely resembling the

Muse. Now, more often than not, I sat at the damned machine as if someone had cut my hands off at the wrists. Three or four times a day I sat here and was victimized by literary heaves. Nothing came. Or if it did, it wound up on the floor in hairballs I swept up every night. I was going through that long desert known as Dry Spell, Arizona.

It had a lot to do with Peg so far away among all those catacomb mummies in Mexico, and my being lonely, and no sun in Venice for the three months, only mist and then fog and then rain and then fog and mist again. I wound myself up in cold cotton batting each midnight and rolled out all fungus at dawn. My pillow was moist every morning, but I didn't know what I had dreamed to salt it that way.

I looked out the window at that telephone, which I listened for all day every day, which never rang offering to bank my splendid novel if I could finish it last year.

I saw my fingers moving on the typewriter keys, fumbling. I thought they looked like the hands of the dead stranger in the cage, dangled out in the water moving like sea anemones, or like the hands, unseen, of the man behind me tonight on the train.

Both men gestured.

Slowly, slowly, I sat down.

Something thumped within my chest like someone bumping into the bars of an abandoned cage.

Someone breathed on my neck....

I had to make both of them go away. I had to do something to quiet them so I could sleep.

A sound came out of my throat as if I were about to be sick. But I didn't throw up.

Instead, my fingers began to type, x-ing out the UNTITLED NOVEL until it was gone.

Then I went down a space and saw these words begin to jolt out on the paper: DEATH and then IS A and then LONELY and then, at last, BUSINESS.

I grimaced wildly at the title, gasped, and didn't stop typing for an hour, until I got the storm-lightning train rolled away in the rain and let the lion cage fill with black sea water which poured forth and set the dead man free....

Down and through my arms, along my hands, and out my cold fingertips onto the page.

In a flood, the darkness came.

I laughed, glad for its arrival.

And fell into bed.

As I tried to sleep, I began sneezing and sneezing and lay miserably using up a box of Kleenex, feeling the cold would never end.

During the night the fog thickened, and way out in the bay somewhere sunk and lost, a foghorn blew and blew again. It sounded like a great sea beast long dead and heading for its own grave away from shore, mourning along the way, with no one to care or follow.

During the night a wind moved in my apartment window and stirred the typed pages of my novel on the desk. I heard the paper whisper like the waters in the canal, like the breath on my neck, and at last I slept.

I awoke late to a blaze of sun. I sneezed my way to the door and flung it wide to step out into a blow of daylight so fierce it made me want to live forever, and so ashamed of the thought, I wanted, like Ahab, to strike the sun. Instead I dressed quickly. My clothes from last night were still damp. I put on tennis shorts and a jacket, then turned the pockets of my damp coat out to find the clot of papier-mâché that had fallen from the dead man's suit only a few hours ago.

I touched the pieces with my fingernail, exhaling. I knew what they were. But I wasn't ready to face up to it yet.

I am not a runner. But I ran....

Away from the canal, the cage, the voice talking darkness on the tram, away from my room and the fresh pages waiting to be read which had started to say it all, but I did not want to read them yet. I just ran blindly south on the beach.

Into Lost World country.

I slowed at last to stare at the forenoon feedings of strange mechanical beasts.

Oil wells. Oil pumps.

These great pterodactyls, I said to friends, had arrived by air, early in the century, gliding in late nights to build their nests. Startled, the shore people woke to hear the pumping sounds of vast hungers. People sat up in bed wakened by the creak, rustle, stir of skeletal shapes, the heave of earthbound, featherless wings rising, falling like primeval breaths at three a.m. Their smell, like time, blew along to shore, from an age before caves or the men who hid in caves, the smell of jungles falling to be buried in earth and ripening to oil. I ran through this forest of brontosauri, imagining triceratops, and the picket-fence stegosaurus, treading black syrups, sinking in tar. Their laments echoed from the shore, where the surf tossed back their ancient thunders.

I ran past the little white cottages that came later to nest among the monsters, and the canals that had been dug and filled to mirror the bright skies of 1910 when the white gondolas sailed on clean tides and bridges strung with firefly lightbulbs promised future promenades that arrived like overnight ballet troupes and ran away never to return after the war. And the dark beasts just went on sucking the sand while the gondolas sank, taking the last of some party's laughter with them.

Some people stayed on, of course, hidden in shacks or locked in some few Mediterranean villas thrown in for architectural irony.

Running, I came to a full halt. I would have to turn back in a moment and go find that papier-mâché mulch and then go seek the name of its lost and dead owner.

But for now, one of the Mediterranean palaces, as blazing white as a full moon come to stay upon the sands, stood before me.

"Constance Rattigan," I whispered. "Can you come out and play?"

It was, in fact, a fiery white Arabian Moorish fortress facing the sea and daring the tides to come in and pull it down. It had minarets and turrets and blue and white tiles tilted precariously on the sand-shelves no more than one hundred feet from where the curious waves bowed to do obeisance, where the gulls circled down for a chance look, and where I stood now taking root.

"Constance Rattigan."

But no one came out.

Alone and special in this thunder-lizard territory, this palace guarded that special cinema queen.

A light burned in one tower window all night and all day. I had never seen it not on. Was she there now?

Yes!

For the quickest shadow had crossed the window, as if someone had come to stare down at me and gone away, like a moth.

I stood remembering.

Hers had been a swift year in the Twenties, with a quick drop down the mine shaft into the film vaults. Her director, old newsprint said, had found her in bed with the studio hairdresser, and cut Constance Rattigan's leg muscles with a knife so she would no longer be able to walk the way he loved. Then he had fled to swim straight west toward China. Constance Rattigan was never seen again. If she could walk no one knew.

God, I heard myself whisper.

I sensed that she had ventured forth in my world late nights and knew people I knew. There were breaths of near meetings between us.

Go, I thought, bang the brass lion knocker on her shorefront door.

No. I shook my head. I was afraid that only a black-and-white film ectoplasm might answer.

You do not really want to meet your special love, you only want to dream that some night she'll step out and walk, with her footprints vanishing on the sand as the wind follows, to your apartment where she'll tap on your window and enter to unspool her spirit-light in long creeks of film on your ceiling.

Constance, dear Rattigan, I thought, run out! Jump in that big white Duesenberg parked bright and fiery in the sand, rev the motor, wave, and motor me away south to Coronado, down the sunlit coast!

No one revved a motor, no one waved, no one took me south to sun, away from that foghorn that buried itself at sea.

So I backed off, surprised to find salt water up over my tennis shoes, turned to walk back toward cold rain in cages, the greatest writer in the world, but no one knew, just me.

This 1952 cookbook excerpt reminds us that once upon a time Americans outside California needed instruction in avocado-eating. It also touts a commercial brand name, cluttering up a centuries-long worldwide debate about what to call the fruit. A hundred years ago, the choices were: alligator pear (deplored in California), *aguacate* (a Spanish Royal Academy mash-up), and *ahuacate*, used in California until the US Department of Agriculture threw its weight behind "avocado," coined in Jamaica in the seventeenth century (and popularized by its use as a Pearl Jam album title). The recipe is from Helen Evans Brown's *West Coast Cookbook*, one of twelve she published from 1946 to 1964, writing about fresh local ingredients, patio dining, and Mexican and Asian cooking. She was the culinary compadre of James Beard (their correspondence was published as *Love and Kisses and a Halo of Truffles*) and a legendary cookbook collector. By using the growers' brand name, Brown also dodges the question of which of the 1,000 varieties of avocado (per the University of California database) to buy or grow.

NATURE NOTE 3
BRANDING

AVOCADOS

HELEN EVANS BROWN

WHY THE AVOCADO WAS SO LONG IN COMING TO California is a mystery. Mexico has always given generously of her secrets of good food, and it has been a favorite there since the days of the Aztecs. Actually, though, it wasn't until 1871 that Judge Ord, of Santa Barbara, was really successful in raising them in California and not until 1924, when the Growers Exchange was formed, that the avocado began to be generally known.

Henry E. Huntington was one of the famous Californians who gave the avocado a boost on its road to fame. He was served one at Los Angeles's Jonathan Club, and was so intrigued that he pocketed the seed and took it home to plant in his fabulous gardens in San Marino. That was the beginning of the avocado grove at the world-renowned Henry E. Huntington Library. Today, at least on the West Coast, the avocado is accepted as casually as the tomato or the onion, and we are always in the midst of working out new recipes for its use. The growers' cooperative, which has dubbed its avocados "Calavos" [a brand name], will allow only fourteen of the ninety-nine common varieties to bear that label and, besides, their fruit must meet other high standards. An avocado by any other name may taste as good, but not necessarily so. To be a Calavo it has to be good.

Avocados are at their best when eaten fully ripe. We have learned that it is better to purchase them when they are still hard and ripen them at home at a temperature of between fifty-five and seventy degrees—this because thought-less marketers will test an avocado's ripeness with careless thumbs that leave it bruised and discolored for later purchasers. Harassed green-grocers have been known to display a coconut near their stock of avocados, with the sug-gestion that those with an urge to pinch use it! Avocados are properly tested for ripeness in two ways: If the seed rattles inside, they are almost ripe; if they give slightly when pressed between the palms of both hands (gently!), they are ready to eat. An avocado is most easily peeled by cutting it through the middle, as you would a peach, then stripping off the skin. If only half is to be used, leave the pit in the remaining portion and rub the cut surface with butter or lemon juice to prevent discoloration.

Connoisseurs prefer the avocado on the half shell, with salt, or the juice of lemon or lime, or possibly with a tarter-than-usual French dressing. Another way they approve is to serve it with a decanter of light rum and with halves of lime, allowing the guests to add each in judicious amounts—this for a first course or a dessert. To sweeten or not to sweeten is a controversial subject; most gourmets believe that the avocado loses in the act. However, avocado ice cream is popular and good. But as for cooking the fruit, all experts agree that it is ruinous. Not only does the magnificent flavor of the avocado disappear entirely, a distasteful one takes its place. However, the avocado may be added to many cooked dishes just before serving—warming it does it no harm. And so we add them, diced, to creamed chicken or crab meat or lobster, we fold them into mashed potatoes, or add them to consommé or tomato bisque. We serve them on the half shell, as a cup for jellied madrilène, and some of us use them as a receptacle for crab meat, or salad, or fruit cocktail, or even caviar.

Avocado Salad

Avocados on the half shell, their centers filled with a dressing made with ½ cup each of wine vinegar and olive oil, and two tablespoons each of minced parsley, green pepper, and green onions, is a fine dish, either as a first course or as a salad.

Dressing
½ cup wine vinegar
½ cup olive oil
2 tablespoons minced parsley
2 tablespoons minced green pepper
2 tablespoons minced green onion

PHOTO BY ANN SUMMA

It's one of the great surprises of young adulthood to discover that your parents or grandparents may have been interesting at one point in their lives. Young themselves, even. Whether it's a photo of great-grandma wearing a cloche hat, a copy of a Ban the Bomb speech written by grandpa in the 1950s, or a tale told by your very own parent, proof of one's ancestors being part of larger history can also be a secret door to a city's life story. Here are two examples from a monthly column that ran in *Westways* magazine in the late 1990s. In it, writers of various ages and backgrounds researched and/or interviewed their parents, focusing on some part of their story that unfolded in a particular place in Southern California. "My Father's Malibu," about events circa 1959, and "My Mother's Griffith Park," remembering 1968, were both originally published in 1997. Both also happen to illuminate chapters in the so-called post–World War II "youth culture" era.

YOUNG PARENTS DOUBLE TAKES

MY FATHER'S MALIBU (1959)

COLLEEN DUNN BATES

LONG BEFORE RECOVERED MEMORY BECAME THE RAGE, I spent many adolescent hours straining to remember my toddlerhood. It was not scenes of abuse I sought, however, but a hipness so profound, I ached to know it better. I had been present on the Malibu surf scene of the fifties—a concept cool beyond belief to a thirteen-year-old L.A. surfer girl in 1971—but I could remember none of it. Because by the time I turned three, in the dawn of the sixties, my father had abandoned Malibu for family and career.

You'd never have pegged the young Joe Dunn for a future Malibu surfer. Pale, freckle-faced, and asthmatic, he grew up in Los Feliz, where he was an altar boy, model airplane builder, and overprotected youngest child. But his world broadened in 1952, when he started at Loyola University and became friends with Terry Connolly, whose screenwriter father owned a little house in the Malibu Colony. Connolly had a surfboard, and my father was fascinated. Then, as now, the real action was at Surfrider (dubbed the 'Bu), the public beach between Malibu Point and the pier, just south of the private Malibu Colony Drive. In those days, when boards were heavy and leashes hadn't been invented, surfers consisted of a handful of he-man lifeguard types competing for the point-break waves. There was a Hollywood contingent, led by Peter Lawford; some famed big-wave riders, such as Walter Hoffman; and such heroes of the sport as Pete Peterson, the captain of the Santa Monica lifeguards.

Intimidated by the talent and competitiveness, my father and his friends headed north in the winter of '53 to deserted Point Dume. They knocked out the rear windows of their cars to haul the balsa-and-redwood boards, which were typically at least ten feet long and upwards of fifty pounds. They wore black, skintight navy-surplus wool sweaters against the cold water, and knee-paddled into wave after wave until they had mastered the basics.

Soon thereafter they found a home: a vacant lot on Old Malibu Road just north of the Colony, in a neighborhood of rickety homes set on pilings. Sandwiched between two houses, the lot was mostly an ice plant–covered slope leading down to a soft sand beach. It was empty and unused—and, best of all, the rocks and sand under the swelling sea created a rideable surf break. They named the spot Little Beach, built a low-slung palm-frond hut in which to escape the sun by day and stash boards by night, and surfed every chance they got.

Word got around, and the scene grew; sometimes as many as a hundred people would crowd the small stretch of sand, drinking beer and commenting on every wave. Although it never had the cachet of the 'Bu (home to Miki Dora and a teenage girl nicknamed Gidget), it seems to me that Little Beach must have been unspeakably cool. A young painter named Billy Al Bengston became a regular, as did a brash actor named Dickie Jaeckel, who had played in the movie *Sands of Iwo Jima*. My father organized the annual Duke Dunn Luau, a wild affair that was forced to move to a new location each year, since the previous party always left behind angry parents or neighbors.

By 1956, my father was working hard as a real estate broker; in 1957, he married; and in 1958, I came along. Sometimes he still rose before daylight to ride the waves before work, and on weekends he'd haul my new baby sister and me to Little Beach, where one of the crowd would watch us while he surfed. When baby number three was born in 1960, he traded in the Malibu outings for family vacations at rented houses in Capistrano Beach.

Thirty-seven years later, I met my father at his downtown office and we set off for PCH. Despite the intervening decades, he found Little Beach right away, still a vacant lot between two beach houses. (In the mid-sixties, geologists had deemed the land unbuildable.) The ice plant is gone, replaced by chain link, scrubby beach trees, and vines, and when we got down to the sand, Dad was taken aback at how erosion had eaten the already-small beach. But the surf break was just as he remembered it, and a small swell was running. We paddled out and shared a dozen fun waves. We're thinking of making it a habit.

MY MOTHER'S GRIFFITH PARK (1968)

ERIC GUTIERREZ

MY MOTHER, NORMA JEAN, IS TWENTY-SIX; MY BROTHER, David, is nine. I'm about to turn eight. We're freshly divorced, surrounded by hippies, and free in Eden. It's a "happening" in Griffith Park, and the smile we share is huge.

On our earlier visits, we stood out as refugees from the Chicano Establishment. Hard-soled shoes and neat parts in our hair. We attended the happenings like church. They had a lot in common: long hours, strange music, hugging crowds, and an emphasis on peace and love. All over America, the children of Eisenhower were taking to the parks and the streets, braless and shoeless to celebrate or to protest. For us, the happenings were a celebration of being young, of awakening power, of a future we would make different from our past. The same things that brought people together at happenings and love-ins across the country, I suppose.

The happenings took place in a field near the park's merry-go-round. Winding through the hills from the Valley side, crammed in my aunt Cookie's cherry red '64 Mustang, we sang "If I Had a Hammer," harmonizing harder as the tie-dyed crowd came into view. Our mother took us to ride the bobbing wooden horses or small-gauge train along the lip of the park, but we couldn't wait to race back to the grassy field. Soon we abandoned rides completely. Given a choice between a happening or Disneyland, we all would have ditched Mickey for a psychedelic summer afternoon in Griffith Park, where the stench of patchouli first nauseated me and I saw my inaugural naked man and woman.

"The happenings were a place where I could be with people my own age, even though I had kids, and not have to spend any money," my mother remembers. "It was a full day of entertainment. And no matter what they say now, it wasn't about sex and drugs. You could trust people. You could just leave your bag or shoes someplace, and you knew they would be there when you came back. For the afternoon, everyone was part of the family."

Our family was changing in Griffith Park. My aunt braided a feather into my mother's hair one afternoon. She had never looked more beautiful.

David and I learned much from the hippies. Like how to cool off by breaking sprinkler heads, then using the soggy grass and mud as a slippery slide. How to flash the peace sign. How to play a Jew's harp. We hiked the surrounding trails, sometimes stumbling upon the makeshift campsites of those my mother reverently called "flower children," as if they were some delicate, mythical race temporarily lost among us. We learned how to make dandelion chains. We petted parrots and snakes and an ocelot. Our hair grew so that it couldn't hold a part.

"The park was always clean," my mother recalls. "No one abused anything, sprayed graffiti, or broke bottles. No one would allow it. Too many bare feet. Everyone wore velvet or lace, and there were so many fresh flowers; it made me think of what it might have been like in old Mexico, just mingling with all sorts of people in the town square."

Adults painted each other's faces (my mother drew the line at letting strangers paint us); played dulcimers, drums, and guitars; and broke into wild, interpretive dances with an abandon that embarrassed and excited us. David and I were tempted by the free food, especially the sodas and peanut-butter-and-jelly sandwiches on the spongy supermarket bread we craved, but we knew better to even ask. Our mother would not hear of "communist dining." We ate corn tortillas from respectable brown bags, sitting in the paltry shade of the smaller trees on the edge of the sixties.

"You could leave a small donation if you wanted to or eat for free," my mother remembers more charitably now. "It was only one or two tables with food, but there was always enough. Everyone shared, and you got the feeling of the miracle of the loaves and fishes."

We got kites after seeing them floating above the park's sun-charred hills. Panorama City had too many overhead power lines for kites, but Griffith Park was wide open. My heart raced when they finally took flight. But what I remember above all is the sight of my mother, releasing more string and running barefoot as fast as she could through a summer of love.

Grit & Glamour, Boyle Heights, 2010

L.A. CIUDAD
DANNY MARTINEZ

The geographic elements that encompass the Southern California area become deep-rooted in our psyches. No doubt, it's a special gift if you hail from here. The mountains to one side, the blue Pacific to the other. And between the crashing waves and the foothills are the grit, glamour, blood, sweat, and tears that make this place fucking amazing. Add the atmospheric swirls of car exhaust, salty ocean mist, pissed alleyways, freshly burnt marijuana, and bacon-wrapped hot dogs—all staples of this great metropolis.

East Los Angeles cradled me; South Central Los Angeles raised me. The 1992 Uprising showed a ten-year-old kid just how vile and passionate Angelenos can be. As some of my childhood friends found crews and gangs and guns to shoot, I found myself with a different weapon of choice. The urban landscape and eclectic mixture of cultures provide a great palette to work from. Going out and attempting to capture the pulse and rhythm of "La Ciudad" is an experience that changes in myriad ways—just as the city does.

—D.M.

Melting L.A., Sixth Street Bridge, 2012

Flowering on Spring, Music Center steps, 2015

Pipe Dreams, Angeles Forest Highway, 2013

May Day, Downtown L.A., 2012

Central Patterns, Central Avenue between Seventh and Eighth streets, 2011

L.A. River, First Street Bridge with Fourth Street and Sixth Street bridges behind, 2011

Two Giants, Downtown L.A., 2011

Sombrero y Botas, L.A. Chinatown, 2010

Santa Monica Wheel, Santa Monica, 2010

Calaveras, DTLA during Art Walk, 2010

Architect Wendy Gilmartin's mission to draw new audiences into a conversation about "a more meaningful understanding of the city and its physical manifestations" got a big boost in 2011, when she launched her Fugly Buildings blog for *LA Weekly*. With humor, deft language, and a loving, unsentimental understanding of the hows and whys of building and urban development in her native city, she roamed the world outside the enclaves of high architecture to tell Angelenos more about the built stuff we have to look at, drive past, worship in, and do business in the vicinity of every day.

SO FUGLY SEEN NEARBY

THE BANK THAT LOOKS LIKE A DEL TACO

WENDY GILMARTIN

Wells Fargo branch, 6348 Sepulveda Blvd., Van Nuys, July 12, 2012

at this Wells Fargo branch in Van Nuys, but, sadly, you probably aren't gonna get one.

Built in 2007 where a Mobil gas station used to sit at the corner of Victory and Sepulveda boulevards, this fairly new, ketchup-and-mustard-colored building could fool any stoner cruising for munchies late at night through the San Fernando Valley.

In the fifties and sixties (and, with a few exceptions, into the seventies), Los Angeles banks built modernist, monolithic neighborhood branch buildings that stood out solidly among a variety of other types and scales of commercial developments like strip malls and car washes, etc. Certain banks, like California-based Home Savings, even commissioned local artists to create murals and sculptures that are considered by some conservationist groups to be local, historical artifacts that deserve protecting.

These mausoleum-like financial institutions were heavy on the outside, silent and too cold with air-conditioning on the inside. They were discrete environments of hushed seriousness where, upon stepping inside past the heavy metal-and-glass doors and leaving the hum of the traffic on the street, you knew there was important business going on in there.

These days, whatever the branch or franchise-based corporate business—be it a McDonald's, a Starbucks drive-through, Verizon, Blockbuster (yes, they still exist), Bank of America, Wells Fargo, or Del Taco—it seems the primary-colored stucco box is every suit's first choice when it comes to showing their brick-and-mortar face to the public. What gets communicated to the public is this: Cheaper is better, and L.A. gets one more fugly building in an increasingly homogenous landscape of other Del Taco banks.

We're guessing the red-and-yellow palette here at 6348 Sepulveda is derived from the Wells Fargo logo—although this building sports a brick red and wimpy shade of custard more than a crimson and gold. The signs and stucco have faded so unevenly that what's left is a pinkish/burnt-orange mess, not that it was ever beautiful to begin with. The building gets no help, either, from the strangely hovering red boxes above each window and doorway (that contain downlighting) or from the pathetic metal trellises that grow nothing on the south and west sides of the building because they're baking in the scorching Valley sun all afternoon.

THE ZIPPER ON A PANTS SUIT

Harmony Gold Theater and Offices, 7655 Sunset Blvd., Hollywood, September 4, 2012

a dated throwback to Hollywood's swinging mid-to-late-century heyday, and just like exposed chest hair and copious gold chains, the "Harmony GOLD" signage out front really completes the look on this groovy geezer. (Blink too fast and you might mistake the sign for the classic "Solid Gold" logo.)

Built in 1965 in the midst of an experimental-building explosion by a handful of local architects (namely Gin Wong's LAX Theme structure in 1961, John Lautner's Sheats/Goldstein house in 1962, Welton Becket's Cinerama Dome in 1963, and Irving Shapiro's Columbia Savings bank in 1965), 7655 Sunset maybe tried to play along with the bold formal gestures, colors, and artful engineering of its peers by offering an overly obvious asymmetry and swoopy, scale-less plain-stucco skin that burrito-wraps the theater. The fused-on, straitlaced other half of the building fills out the lot to the corner of Stanley Avenue.

The "Harmony Gold" building is actually a multipurpose complex that houses offices for the distribution and production wing of Harmony Gold's movie, TV, and animation business (it is the sole license holder of the eighties Robotech anime franchise and all its spin-offs, and coproduced the epic *Shaka Zulu* TV miniseries, circa 1986); offices for the strangely, and seemingly unrelated, property management side of the Harmony business; offices for lease for anybody else; and a state-of-the-art, 350-seat theater for DGA and SAG screenings, plus adjoining spaces for private events. All of it sits on top of a subterranean, structured parking lot.

As for the heavy-topped, taupe-shaped theater block on the left side that recalls Donald Trump's cast-in-place coiffure, we get it—they show movies inside, and windows don't work in a screening space. But take Westwood's now-demolished National theater (built in 1970) for a better example of a successful design in a similarly functioning space. Yes, from a certain angle, the beloved National looked like a brown-stucco blob eating a window façade, but the place opened itself up to the street so drivers and pedestrians on Gayley and Lindbrook could look up into the upper and lower lobbies at all the moviegoers milling around inside. Kind of like an ant farm. The National really accentuated its corner location and turned itself into a public show. Despite its primo location, 7655 Sunset gives nothing back to the street. Instead, Harmony Gold's thirty-foot-tall stucco smear going right straight down the front face of the building just sits there like a giant zipper on a pants suit, gingerly holding the whole ensemble together.

118

PHOTO BY DANNY MARTINEZ

Gina B. Nahai's novel *Moonlight on the Avenue of Faith*, about a family spinning out centrifugally from its longtime home, Tehran, is a tricky book. "I couldn't put it down!" is the reader-review refrain, and it's true—even while you tell yourself you'll just stay up to read one more chapter (after all, it's not technically a thriller or a mystery), you have to keep going. Perhaps the secret lies in the fact that although it's often pegged "magic realism," *Moonlight* might be better understood as springing from the *Arabian Nights* tradition of linked fairy tales and stories. Those fairy tale instances of exaggerated cruelty, abrupt transitions, and charmed states work beautifully in an epic diaspora story—what immigrant family history isn't peopled with mythic figures and awe-inspiring events? And indeed, Nahai has based her book on true-life stories shared by her relatives and friends. The Los Angeles where her characters are reunited is uncannily suited to the tale. Here, the action unfolds in settings— like a movie-star mansion where there's never any food in the fridge—that share an implausible plausibility with many a stop on a magic-carpet ride.

LOST & FOUND

GLOBAL FAMILY

MOONLIGHT ON THE AVENUE OF FAITH

GINA B. NAHAI

IN LOS ANGELES, ROCHELLE WENT TO THE AIRPORT TO MEET Miriam and Mister Charles. She watched them get off the TWA jetliner— Miriam wearing the same brown jacket and wing-tip shoes she had put on at the start of her escape from Iran, Mr. Charles dragging his feet behind her, carrying all his worldly belongings in a brown-and-green-check carry-on bag he was ready to defend with his life. Instead of feeling excited to see them, Rochelle felt embarrassed.

In her Chanel suit and her snakeskin pumps, her lips amber and lined with brown pencil, her eyelashes weighted down by too many layers of mascara applied too early in the morning, she rushed up to Miriam, hoping no one she knew was at the airport that morning, and hugged her. Then she ushered her and Mr. Charles to the parking lot and squeezed them both into the one-passenger seat of her convertible Mercedes.

They drove to a rented apartment in a high-rise along Wilshire Boulevard in Westwood. Here, Rochelle told Miriam, many Iranian Jews were living "temporarily" while they awaited the demise of the revolution and the return of the monarchy to Iran.

"They're going to have to wait a very long time," Miriam remarked dryly.

The building was crowded and badly managed and overrun by the smells of ethnic cooking and the noise of moving dollies loading and unloading on every floor. But Miriam moved into her apartment and accepted her exile without illusions. She made a point of going from door to door and meeting all her neighbors, even the Americans, she said, because, after all, it was their country she had come to conquer. The first week, she bought new birds for Mr. Charles and turned their balcony into a small greenhouse where he could grow his plants and flowers. Then she allowed Rochelle to take her on a guided tour of Los Angeles.

In her man's suit jacket and with her shirtsleeves rolled up to her elbow, Miriam the Moon paraded up and down the streets of Beverly Hills, through Rodeo Drive, where Rochelle, who had spent a fortune trying to impress the store clerks into showing her some level of respect, made the mistake of taking her. Miriam fingered the clothes as if she were buying live sheep, asking prices only to tell the clerks everything was too expensive. She demanded to see every manager in every store, warned them—with their impassive faces and asinine looks—against the wrath of Almighty once He looked down upon "this street that's only as long as a donkey's penis" and took notice of the kind of injustice they were creating in this world: asking the sum of a country's gross national product in return for a shirt that was not even silk, not even hand sewn, and that would cost eighteen dollars—eighteen dollars at three thousand Iranian rials to a dollar, the equivalent of a month's rent for a family of five in downtown Iran—every time the shirt needed to be dry-cleaned.

Mortified by her sister's attacks on the holy houses of Gucci and Ferragamo, certain that she would never again be received with anything more than a mocking smile anywhere along Rodeo Drive, Rochelle nudged Miriam away from the street and offered to buy her an ice cream cone, only to have her lecture the pot-smoking teenager behind the counter about the kind of waste he was creating on this planet—selling thirty flavors of ice cream when one would do just as well.

Rochelle took Miriam, with her ladderlike body and her Elvis Costello glasses, to Westwood Boulevard, where the Iranian grocery stores and restaurants were just beginning to open their doors and where Miriam declared she would not step—prices were so much higher than their competitors' on Pico and Fairfax.

Once Miriam settled in, she took two-hour walks on Ocean Avenue every afternoon just for the sake of running into recent Iranian émigrés, and in no time at all she came to know every wino and drug dealer who ever haunted Santa Monica. Convinced as always that wasting food was the great sin known to man, she brought leftover food to her new friends: three-day-old rice with dill and parsley, sautéed lamb shank with onions and garlic and saffron, Cornish hens stuffed with currants and cumin. She carried the food in large pots wrapped in bleached-white cheesecloth that she tied in a knot, so that from far away the pots looked like coddled infants, or the heads of fat women wearing scarves.

Rochelle felt disgraced by Miriam's habits and Sussan complained that she was impossible to please, but no one who had ever known Miriam could deny her unequaled talent for studying people and discerning their secrets. With radarlike instincts, an incomparable memory, and a total lack of respect for the concepts of privacy or subtlety, she came to know the story of every Jew who lived on California's soil and, in time, that of his forebears.

But neither her escape from Iran nor her takeover of Los Angeles would really grant Miriam any degree of satisfaction until she had achieved the task she had set up for herself before leaving Iran: to find me in America, nine years after my father had sent me away with the deliberate purpose of hiding me from my mother's family.

In the end, of course, she did.

WHEN SHE CALLED me that morning from the public phone opposite Mercedez the Movie Star's house, Miriam the Moon introduced herself as "your Dear Auntie Miriam. The one who raised your mother. You probably don't remember me, but I know everything about you, even things you never imagined could be true."

It was August 1981. I had spent three consecutive summers in Mercedez's house. I had come here in early June. Shortly after that, Mercedez had left on one of her spur-of-the moment trips to the Caribbean—the guest of a wealthy old man who claimed to have his own island. The winter before, he had taken her to his 6,000-square-foot house on the slopes of Aspen Mountain.

"Go to your window and look outside," Miriam continued without giving me a chance to catch my breath.

My heart sank to the ground. I bolted out of bed and carried the phone to the window. There she was, at the phone booth on the corner of Sunset and Foothill—a long, dark figure on an empty street in the early-morning quiet, waving at me as she spoke.

"You wouldn't know this," Miriam went on, "but I've been traveling up and down the state of California searching for you."

She was looking straight at my window, as if she could see me standing there, trying to decide if she were a figment of my imagination.

"We had to escape Iran, Mister Charles and I. Mister Charles is my husband. He's from the ghetto, of course, like myself and your mother. But his mother thought she'd given birth to Moses, so she gave him a prince's name: Chaaarles. Never mind she could never pronounce it herself.

"Anyway, nothing doing. He can't even write his own name, much less run a kingdom."

She sighed, indicating this was an old wound she was not going to reopen at that moment outside Mercedez's house.

"During the revolution I went to see your father and asked him for your address and phone number. He wouldn't give them to me. You know how he is. I got to Los Angeles a few months ago. I figured you're of high school age. So I've been going school to school, every public and private high school up and down the state, asking if they have a student by your name. Didn't occur to me to look for Mercedez first, but once I did, there you were. Hang up and open the door. I'll be over in a minute."

With the receiver still in my hand, I watched as the woman hung up at the other end, then bent over and wiped her shoes with a handkerchief she had taken out of her sleeve. She picked up two green woven baskets—the plastic kind women carry to market in third-world countries—and crossed the street without once looking to either side for traffic. I waited 'til she had traversed the yard and stepped up to the door. Then I turned away, face flushed, and wondered what I would do if she ever stepped inside the house.

My first thought when I opened the door was that Miriam was old—much older than Roxanna—and that she bore no trace of a beauty that must have earned her the name Miriam—"as beautiful as"—the Moon. Then I remembered that I had seen her before, that day when she promised me she would find my mother, and even before that, on the few occasions when Miriam had come to the house to deliver bad news or to sit shiva. When I had asked, Roxanna had said yes, Miriam was indeed the most beautiful of all her sisters. She had been prettier than any other girl in their ghetto, outranked only by Mercedez the Movie Star, who had green eyes, but that did not count because Mercedez was the illegitimate child of a Russian aristocrat and an Assyrian phantom.

The woman before me now was unusually tall and thin, legs so long, she looked like a stilt walker in a skirt, her neck so bony, I could see the movement of her Adam's apple as she spoke. She had on a pair of men's wing-tip shoes, a long navy blue skirt, and a brown polyester shirt. Over the shirt she wore a man's gray wool jacket—part of a suit, she would volunteer minutes later, that had once belonged to Mr. Charles. A black polyester scarf was tied in a double knot under her chin. Underneath it her hair, white at the roots, was a Clairol olive at the matted ends. She wore thick spectacles with wide black rims—a gift, she also volunteered, from the relief workers of the UNHCR in Pakistan.

"Miss Lili!" she declared as she walked in and kissed me on both cheeks. She smelled of soap and old clothes. She pulled away and examined my face, then my figure.

"How old are you?" she asked. "Fourteen? Fifteen?"

She shook her head in disappointment.

"You're too thin. You must be one of those girls who like to diet." The word diet sounded like an insult.

Confused and searching for an introduction, I answered that I weighed pretty close to my recommended weight. As stupid as that assertion sounded, Miriam did not seem to find it strange.

"Whoever made that recommendation must be anorexic themselves," she answered. "No wonder you're so pale."

She picked up the baskets she had rested on the floor and headed for Mercedez's kitchen, where the stove had hardly been used.

"That woman must be crazy, leaving you alone in this house with only the maid."

As if aware she was being mentioned, the housekeeper suddenly appeared in the kitchen and stood staring at Miriam in shock.

"Who are you?" she asked.

"This girl's aunt." Miriam did not bother looking at the woman. "You can go mind your own affairs."

She put the baskets on the counter next to the sink, took off her jacket and hung it neatly on the back of a chair, and began to empty strange foods into the refrigerator.

I stood at the open door, one hand still resting on the knob, and watched in disbelief as bottles of rose water and cherry and quince syrup, bags of dried cumin and ground saffron, boxes of halva and dates, bunches of radishes and spinach and grape leaves lined the shelves. Miriam took out two fresh chickens—"Too expensive," she remarked, "but I don't cook if it's not kosher"—and a canvas sack of bleached white rice. "Basmati." She showed me the elephant design printed on the front of the sack. "From India. Persian rice is far superior, of course, but these days you can't get it, even in Iran."

She threw a glance at me from under her glasses and waved with the hand that held a knife.

"You can come in already," she said, motioning toward the breakfast table, where she wanted me to sit. "I know you're a brave little thing, staying in this house all by yourself at night. Don't tell me I scare you that much."

She was opening cabinets, pulling out drawers, rearranging dishes, and learning how to work the stove. She found a bowl and filled it with cold water, soaked a bagful of vegetables I had not seen since the days of my childhood in Iran, and began to sharpen the only kitchen knife by pulling the blade against that of a table knife. Only when she felt I was about to go to the phone and call for help did she bother to explain herself.

"I'm staying all day," she said. "I know that Mercedez wouldn't want me to, that your father doesn't want me to. But you're my niece, I raised your mother, and I intend to get to know you better. So, as long as I'm here and you look like you haven't had a decent meal in years, I figure I should fix you some lunch."

Hours later, we sat down to two kinds of stew and a dish of rice with sweet cherries and saffron chicken. The moment I raised the spoon to my mouth, Miriam threw a glance at my trembling hands and went on the offensive.

"I understand Mercedez has been supporting you."

She said this as a statement of fact, raising her eyebrows to indicate she was not too pleased.

"She and I go way back, and I understand she hasn't changed much since her youth."

Her eyebrows, like my spoon, were still raised.

"If I were your father, I would never have let you come live here or let her pay your way."

She dropped her eyebrows and adjusted herself in her chair. Taking advantage of the momentary lapse in her assault, I swallowed my food and put the spoon back on the plate.

"Anyhow," she continued on a gentler note, "I am here now and we will see much more of each other, and I'll show you how people like us and your mother live."

I put another spoonful of rice in my mouth, swallowed without chewing, never took my eyes off my plate. The mention of my mother had made my heart race. The taste of that food, the smell of the eggplant and the sour raisins, had brought back memories of a place and a time I did not want to revisit.

"I'm still looking for her, you know. One of these days, I'll find her and bring her back."

I remembered Roxanna's hands peeling the thin, long Japanese eggplants, remembered walking with her to the grapevine at the end of the yard, picking the sour grapes coated in dust, eating more than we put in the basket. I remembered her face above the steaming pot of steaming rice, her eyes watching me eat. She had loved me, I thought. I had mattered.

Miriam leaned forward and added some stew to my rice.

"That's why I had to find you first, you see: because I know, sooner or later, Roxanna is going to come back to you."

It shocked me to hear the confidence in Miriam's voice, as if she were speaking not of a fantasy held by an old woman from a strange land but of a widely acknowledged fact.

"Do you still think my mother is alive?" I asked.

I could see my own reflection in the lenses of her glasses—a pair of tiny, identical faces, at once enraged and despondent, aware of their own impotence before this woman who had temporarily disappeared behind her glasses.

"Of course she is." Miriam did not skip a beat. "She's only forty-three years old. Why wouldn't she be alive?"

I felt my stomach turn with anger, felt the food poison my chest and burn through the roof of my mouth.

"Because she's not," I said.

The words had escaped my mouth against my will. It was as if I heard someone else speak, saying things I did not know.

"I know she's not. Everyone knows she's not."

Miriam was shaking her head, rock solid and confident. I realized I hated her.

"No one knows what I know," she said.

In one instant I forgot all the rules of discipline and all the manners taught to me by the nuns, forgot all the methods of self-protection I had learned while living alone, and I lashed out at Miriam, hoping to destroy her.

"You are a stupid woman with stupid thoughts," I yelled, throwing the spoon back onto the plate and watching drops of red stew fly up at Miriam. They stained the lenses of her glasses.

"You didn't know a damn thing even back in Iran when you came to see me."

Miriam remained still, her hands gripping the edge of the table, her eyes strangely calm.

"My mother is dead," I said, and shocked myself again. I wanted to stop, pull back into the same shell of silence and fear I had lived in for ten years. But Miriam was there, and I could not stop myself.

"She killed herself," I screamed. "I watched her do it. She's dead."

The maid had heard my screams and rushed into the kitchen. I stood before Miriam, shocked by what I had said.

"So go away, and take your stinking food with you before Mercedez finds out I ever let you in here."

I walked away from the table, shaking, and leaned on the kitchen counter for balance. I prayed that Miriam would get up and leave, quietly, with the same suddenness with which she had arrived. I prayed that I would forget I ever saw her, that I would not remember what she had said. Most of all, I prayed that she would not find Roxanna.

Miriam the Moon drove the knife in deeper.

"And if she were dead," she asked, wiping her glasses with a tissue and not looking at me, "if your mother were buried somewhere like a dog, would it make it easier for you to understand why she hasn't come back?"

By the time she left that day, Miriam had managed to reinstill in me the same anxiety that had kept me awake all through my childhood. She had cleaned the table and washed the dishes, never allowing the maid past the door and into the kitchen, which had suddenly become Miriam's domain. Carefully, she had labeled the food in the fridge, written down heating instructions for the pots she left on the stove.

"You must come over and meet the family," she had said twice, clearly choosing to ignore my outburst, aware that she had me in her grip. "Rochelle is here, and Sussan, too—with the kids but minus the husband."

I made a face and turned away from her, indicating I was not interested in news of her sisters and their lives. She saw my reaction but went on.

"I'll have a gathering and invite everyone," she went on as if she had not heard me. "Your cousin Josephine is just a few years older than you. Rochelle got her married off as soon as they came to America. She's got two kids already. There're also your great-aunts—your mother's aunts. Dear Auntie Light took a contract out on her husband. The FBI caught her."

For a minute I was stunned. I had seen her—this old woman who had paid to have her husband assassinated by her gardener. I had heard of the incident on the evening news but had not known she was my great-aunt.

"You have to leave," I told Miriam, aware that I was being rude, wanting to be rude. "Mercedez doesn't like me to let weird people in here."

Miriam picked up her plastic baskets and smiled.

"I look weird to you," she declared, again as a statement of fact. "You're going to have to get used to it."

A cyclist on his chopped bike at the 2007 Choppercabras Spring Thing at Atomic Cycles in Van Nuys. Annually for some fifteen years, cyclists on tall bikes, Frankenbikes, and other manipulated machines came to play, compete in demolition derbies, bike joust, and show off.

URBAN
CYCLING
ANN
SUMMA

All my life, I have been a cyclist. A single-speed Schwinn in St. Louis gave me two-wheeled freedom; a touring Raleigh carried me across Europe. I rode a delivery bike in Tokyo; in Silver Lake, I rode my hybrid Nishiki to pieces while trail riding. In the nineties, I rode L.A. County with an all-woman mountain-biking crew. In the first AIDS/LifeCycle ride, a seven day, 600-mile trek from S.F. to L.A., I rode a Greg Lemond Zurich, and in later ALC-rides, a sub-twenty-pound Litespeed. I was road ready.

In 2004, I heard about a "midnight ride" in Echo Park. Jeff and I rode to the Pioneer Market parking lot. People were milling about. Nobody was in spandex; few had helmets. Some women wore high heels or cocktail dresses.

We were nonplussed. Jeff said, "Where are the riders?"

"I think these are them," I answered. It was the second Midnight Ridazz ride.

A cute guy guzzling out of his water bottle offered it to me.

"Want some?" Straight vodka. All righty then.

A leader yelled. We took off whooping down the avenue, around the lake, toward downtown, taking both lanes. Leaders rode ahead and "corked" the intersections, so we rocketed through, regardless of lights. There were almost no cars on the road—but still, the freedom! It was like riding my Schwinn around my Missouri hood.

The Midnight Ridazz grew with each monthly ride, and other urban social rides popped up. I started taking pictures of my biking friends, also doing sessions with the Whirly Girls and with the mechanics at Bicycle Bitchen, a women's repair workshop. It was fabulous to shoot and ride (wearing flapper drag) with the Whirly Girls to Vaginal Davis's Bricktops speakeasy at the Parlour.

Newer, crazier bikes appeared. Frankenbikes, tiny bikes. Choppercabras with plywood sidecars. People built velodromes in their Atwater backyards and held block parties at the Bike Kitchen. The Wolfpack Hustle pushed urban racing and endurance. In East L.A., the Ovarian Psycos Bicycle Brigade began, a new feminist iteration. In Koreatown, Burrito Project cyclists delivered homemade burritos to skid row.

Today, L.A. is becoming a cyclist's dream: dedicated bike lanes, miles of bike paths, Sharrows, the three-foot rule, CicLAvia.

"Cycle tracks will abound in Utopia," said H.G. Wells. We can only hope.

—A.S.

Aurisha Smolarski's bike for the 2005 Echo Park Community Parade is decorated for Christmas. She pedals in her platforms.

Ladylike through the city, Whirly Girls Aurisha Smolarski and Nyrie ride in flapper drag to a WeHo speakeasy, 2004.

A road rider takes a break as a passing bike messenger accelerates.

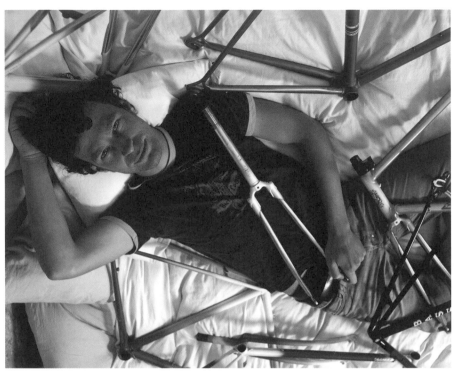

Some cyclists may sleep with their bikes. Transplant Thomas Gotschi with vintage frames from Germany, circa 2006.

Some cyclists give their bikes names.

Whirly Girls are too cool for nobody! They pose at Kim Jensen's apartment before a ride to a 2004 speakeasy night at the Parlour.

The late cyclist known as Tomatoes, a fixture on the bike scene, poses in the Pioneer Market parking lot before a midnight ride.

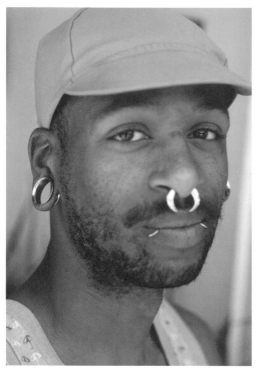

A bike messenger with green cap and piercings.

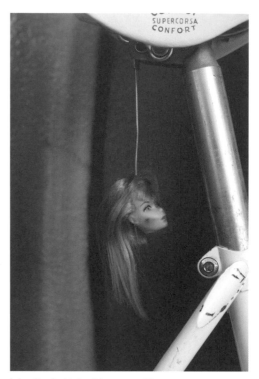

A dangling Barbie head decorates a bike seat.

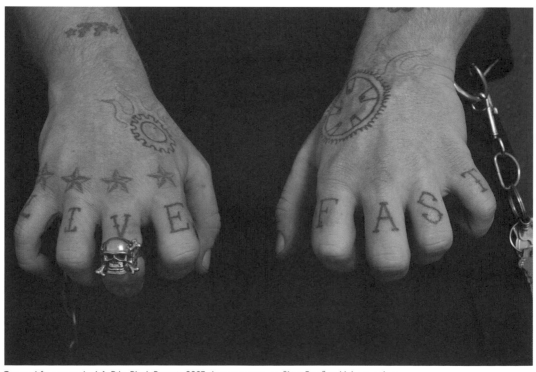

Tattooed fingers at the L.A. Bike Block Party in 2007 show commitment: "Live Fast" and bike sprockets.

Sensible clothes not required. Midnight Ridazz Theater ride in October 2005 stops to socialize and drink.

Portrait of a young man in front of a bike mural at the L.A. Bike Block Party, 2007.

Riders on tall bikes after a bike joust in the San Fernando Valley, June 2007.

This piece is part of a short story about a father and son called "Middle Men," published in a story collection of the same title. Set in the early 2000s, it follows Costello, the father, a salesman for Ajax Plumbing Sales, as he navigates his vast professional territory throughout L.A. County and beyond. Jim Gavin's affectionate, admiring portrait brings attention to a modest man's achievements. The unshowy prose honors his character's seldom-verbalized wit and wisdom. At the same time, memories popping up at moments during each day this week point out deep tectonic tremors of Costello's personal history. Underlying Costello's crisscrossing routes is the weblike geography of the building and goods movement industries that are so vital to Southern California's economy. Although he's still learning to live without his late wife in their suburban Anaheim home, Costello drives the freeways with the satisfaction of long experience, quite at home on his early-morning commute to Compton or headed for sales calls in Baldwin Park and North Long Beach, casual about the trek to a modern mega warehouse in a "paved, semi-incorporated nowhere."

A WEEK
IN THE
LIFE
PATHS

MIDDLE MEN

JIM GAVIN

COSTELLO

Costello sees a lizard at the bottom of the pool. The sucker is dead, dead. Full fathom five, as they say. This lizard situation, on a Saturday, presents a major hassle. Costello stands barefoot on the diving board, bouncing a little, with an unlit Tareyton between his lips. Saturday, an extra layer of brightness, Saturday brightness, like God opening a window in the sky.

The backyard needs some work. Weeds flaming up from cracks in the concrete, all the flower pots empty, the patio cover rotten with termites. Costello pops a net onto the aluminum pole and stands at the edge of the deep end. His wife wanted the deep end extra deep, so the kids could dive. The water is green, the lizard caught in silhouette, his tail wedged underneath the filter cover. Costello scoops up a flotilla of dead june bugs, dumps them in the planter, and then goes deeper, making a play for the lizard.

Next door, Jesse Rocha starts up his hedge trimmer. He's the same age as Costello, but semiretired. By some dull, suburban coincidence Rocha, like Costello, is also a plumbing lifer, but on the skilled side of things, repairs and remodels, three trucks and a shop. Last year, finessing his way out of a worker's comp lawsuit, he changed the company name from Rocha Plumbing to Advanced Plumbing Specialists. "This is the great state of California," he said. "Sunshine and litigation."

Rocha pokes his bald head over the brown cinder-block wall, the same crumbling wall that squares off every yard in this section of Anaheim. He turns off the trimmer.

"Hey, Marty," he says. "I saw that thing in the *Pipeline*. Congratulations."

It came yesterday, the new issue of the *Pipeline*, quarterly organ of the West Coast Plumbing Association. Twelve pages, two staples. Martin Costello, a nominee for sales rep of the year.

"I'm working on my acceptance speech," Costello says.

Rocha laughs. He and Connie are nice enough, always helpful. A common-law thing, no kids. Hedging their bets for twenty years.

"You should hire our pool guy," Rocha says.

"I don't mind doing it."

"Your water looks a little green."

"I'll blow it up with chemicals," Costello says. "Nagasaki the shit out of it." Points to the deep end. "There's a lizard down there. At the bottom."

"I thought lizards could swim."

"I'm not sure."

"Crocodiles can swim," Rocha says. "A crocodile is just a big lizard."

"I know salamanders can swim."

"That's true."

"They're amphibious," Costello says.

"My grandma used to keep axolotls." Rocha spells the word for him. "Mexican salamanders," he explains. "Milky white, with golden eyes. They'd freak you out."

"Golden eyes? Holy shit."

Nods, silence. A meeting of minds. Two medieval doctors.

"You're not swimming, are you?" Rocha asks. "The water's a little green."

"I'm just gonna float around on the raft."

The trimmer cracks on, the noise a million tiny cracks in the afternoon.

Costello is shirtless, his belly soft and pink. Still wearing his old Dodgers cap. He hasn't combed his hair on a Saturday in thirty years, not since before the kids were born. He flips the cap around so he can see what he's doing. The long pole rests against his shoulder; he pushes it under the lizard, but the poor sucker won't budge. Costello gives up.

His sacraments wait for him by the shallow-end steps.

Sports page, crossword puzzle, felt-tip pen, the Tareytons, three left, and a Zippo flashing in the sun. And the new issue of the *Pipeline*. A bit of vanity. He climbs carefully onto the plastic raft and pushes off the side, off the tile that she chose, orange and purple, a floral mosaic, Spanish.

A nice day, warm and clear. What they call an azure sky. On the wooden telephone pole in the corner of the yard, a single crow keeps vigil. The telephone wires run parallel to everything. The sky divided by clean horizontal lines: the roof, the wall, the wires. This is what he paid for. Peaceful ranch house living. Sea-green stucco and a sliding glass door.

Three mortgages, babe, each one more magnificent than the last.

Costello is looking at himself. Page three of the *Pipeline*, a feature article about the company he works for, Ajax Plumbing Sales, of Compton. Special notices to Jack Isahakian, the owner, who is nominated for manager of the year, and to him, Martin Costello, the top outside guy. The supreme council of elders will announce the awards this Friday, after the annual WCPA Best Ball Extravaganza. Every contractor, rep, and wholesaler in SoCal descending on whatever shitball municipal golf course the council has managed to rent out. The hackfest of all hackfests.

Costello is pictured merrily athwart a brand-new Ultima 900, which he specified onto every tract house built last year in the high desert by Progressive Plumbing, Inc. (formerly Lamrock & Hoon LLC). The defective ballcocks on the Ultimas are still causing problems—a nightmare sorting the warranty situation with the factory—but the article doesn't mention that. A nice fluff piece. Jack, in his humility, made the photographer put the entire Ajax crew in the picture, inside sales, outside sales, warehouse crew, everybody hanging off forklifts and pallets in the sunny pipe yard. Everybody squinting, faces bright. Linda—pronounced Leenda—in her wheelchair, waving to the camera. Next to the forklift, Costello's son, Matt, the picture taken a couple weeks before he gave up plumbing to finish his degree, God bless. The article extols Ajax's transformation after the brutalities of the last housing crash, the bust years, 1989–95, the trifecta mortgage years. Jack Isahakian, quoted at length: "We got fat on new construction like everybody else, but when reality set in we had to change things, think smaller, master the nickel and dime stuff with our wholesalers." All the news that's fit to print.

Rocha finishes whacking his bottlebrush plant, turns the trimmer off. Costello, drifting in the deep end, sees a cloud of red needles floating over the wall.

"We're turning on the barbecue tonight," says Rocha. "Feel free to come by."

A year of warm regards and kind invitations. A year of telling lies to avoid them.

"I'm meeting the kids for dinner," says Costello. "Thanks, though."

Rocha salutes and leaves the wall. A moment later the sound of his diving board, then a splash of impressive magnitude. Jesse Rocha, a virtuoso of the cannonball.

Costello lights up. Tareyton, the taste we're fighting for. No more sneaking them. Killing himself out in the open, under a blue sky.

Costello drifts for a few minutes, blowing smoke rings, idly snapping the Zippo. Nice and quiet. A dragonfly hovers over the water, touching down smooth and fast, then gone, zigzagging up and over the wall, a dust-off.

The telephone pole in the corner of the yard, like the mainmast of a ship. Galleons and caravels. Sailors in the crosstrees on lookout. Magellan and his crew, drifting on the equator, praying for wind.

Costello starts the crossword, but can't concentrate. An uneasy feeling clutches his stomach. The lizard directly below, full fathom five. He pushes off toward the shallow end and disembarks, his feet slipping into the slimy water.

Evening comes. The house is dark. Costello drives his Pontiac Grand Am one block, parks in a cul-de-sac, and walks back to the house, slipping in through the side gate. Smoke and mirrors to make the Rochas think he's out with the kids. The Rochas always knock a second time, asking again if he wants to come over.

Later, in his recliner, in the dark, with the air-conditioning blasting, he turns on the game. The voice of Vin Scully, soothing and omniscient, the God voice of SoCal. Costello gets nervous during games. He paces the green shag in the family room, looking for distractions. The upper shelves of the wall unit are full of pictures, Katie and Matt and Megan, as kids, in various stages of toothlessness and rec league glory. Then the encyclopedias, *Funk & Wagnalls*, A through Z, one a month at Safeway for two years. Costello wants to look up axolotls, but "A" is missing. There's a copy of *Moby-Dick*. Some other random books of nautical lore. Krakens, mermaids, the fata morgana. Costello finds the book of explorers, turns to his favorite passage. Magellan's crew, lost in the doldrums of the Pacific, slowly starving to death. Costello, laughing, reads his favorite quote: "…and when they ran out of rats, they chewed the bark off the mainmast."

In the kitchen, by the light of the refrigerator, Costello takes out a giant bag of hot dogs. Then a giant tub of mustard, then a giant tub of mayonnaise. Smart & Final, apocalypse shopping. He puts dogs on a paper plate, shoves them in the microwave. Waiting, he sets up four buns, slapping on mustard and mayonnaise. He takes a fifth bun, balls it up, dips it in the mayonnaise, swallows it whole. The dogs pop and hiss. He pours Pepsi from a two-liter bottle into a clean glass just out of the dishwasher. A bit of decorum. The television illuminates the family room, waves of blue, aquarium light. Costello, leaning forward in his recliner, a dish towel over his knees, eyes focused on the game, mayonnaise punctuating both sides of his mouth, this is how he eats. The kids are trying to get him out more. It's been over a year, they say, you need to get out there, you need to do something, go somewhere. Go where? We've got the pool.

In the bottom of the ninth a pinch hitter stares innocently at strike three. Costello throws his cap at the television, stomps down the dark hall. For a while he plays hearts on the computer, sipping his Pepsi, trying to calm down. His animated opponents are a bear, an alien, and some kind of go-go dancer. At ten o'clock, hearing the Disneyland fireworks. He can't help himself. He goes out through the garage, scales the side gate onto the roof, and walks barefoot across the asphalt shingles. An old summer ritual, watching fireworks on the roof, his pool and Rocha's sparkling in the darkness, the kids tossing their Popsicle sticks down the chimney. He lights up, snaps the Zippo. Down below he sees Rocha and Connie, holding beers, watching the sky. They hear something, start looking around. Connie, ten years younger than Rocha, firm as all hell, what they call a biker babe. Thou shalt not covet. Soon they'll notice the man lurking above them. They will ask legitimate questions and listen generously to his implausible answers. This is bad form, weird and selfish behavior, blowing them off to watch the game alone. They are nice enough people.

Costello, on tiptoe, moves toward the chimney, the only hiding place, but he trips on one of the support wires that hold up the old TV aerial. He rolls down the slant, but the chimney catches him before he can plunge into the dead rosebushes. Cursing silently to himself, he hears Rocha.

"Marty? Is that you?"

"Marty, are you okay?" Connie calls in her raspy voice. Costello crouches behind the chimney. A night ambush. The sky cracking, turning colors. Surrender.

"Yeah," he says, standing up, faking laughter. "I tripped."

"Don't fall off the roof, man," Rocha says.

"Look," Costello says, pointing in the general direction of the Matterhorn. "Here comes the grand finale."

Greens and blues and reds, whirling and cracking. Connie claps when it's over.

"I'll see you Friday, Marty," Rocha says, squeezing Connie's ass.

"You will?"

"The WCPA tourney," Rocha reminds him.

"Right," Costello says. "Ajax is sponsoring a hole. Stop by if you want."

An hour later, with his bloody foot wrapped in toilet paper, he watches the local news, waiting for sports and weather.

Sunday, Costello arrives late to evening mass, sits in the back, falls asleep during the homily, then slips out right after Communion, still chewing the wafer as he hurries across the parking lot. Francine, the parish retard, accosts him. Forty going on ten. Not enough oxygen to the brain at birth. Acne, hairy upper lip, one of God's defectives. Lives in a halfway house down the street. She rides around on a beach cruiser, greeting people, keeping track of who goes to mass, spreading her tragic brand of glee. His wife was friends with Francine, or put up with her, at least, let her stop by the house, let her ramble on and on. For a while, afterward, Francine came by to visit Costello. He'd hold the door half closed, smile, feign sleep, illness, never letting her in. A responder to subtle hints Francine is not.

She rolls toward him on her bike.

"Hi, Marty!"

"Hey, there, Francine," Costello says, swallowing the consecrated host. "Shouldn't you be wearing a helmet?"

Keys, door, faster. A fucking zombie attack.

"Bye, Marty!"

• • •

On Monday morning Costello neatly arranges his hair crosswise over his skull using a comb, a blow dryer, and an aerosol product called "The Dry Look." Pleated khakis, beige golf shirt with Ajax logo, brown Members Only jacket. Everything you own is brown, she said. He clicks the Nextel into his belt holster and leaves the house at six o'clock.

Anaheim is beautiful. Supremo freeway access in all directions. All that concrete crisscrossing in the air, north and south, east and west, a compass rose. He takes the 91, the Artesia Freeway, east toward the Ajax warehouse in Compton. The freeway all to himself. Dick Dale on cassette, black coffee from McDonald's, a trunk full of defective ballcocks. He checks the odometer: 237,000 and counting. He averages 50,000 miles per year, vast territories, circles of latitude, Inglewood to Barstow, sailing across SoCal, all day, every day. Thirty-five years, carry the one, that's a couple million miles. Circumnavigation. Begin where you end, end where you begin. Sailors crossing the equator, initiated into the ancient mysteries of the deep. Getting laid in the watery parts of the world. In Hong Kong, R&R, the house on the hill, his first and only piece before her. Fifty thousand miles per year. Let them bury Martin Costello on the freeway. Let them throw his body over the side of a transition loop, commending his soul to *Trafficus rex*.

He exits the 91, cruises down Avalon Boulevard, turns left into an industrial cul-de-sac. Pigeons and graffiti and concertina wire. Costello parks next to Jack Isahakian's Mercury Grand Marquis. Luis, the Lord of Will Call, walks out of the Ajax warehouse, on his way to get breakfast at the roach coach, which has entered the cul-de-sac, horn blaring. The sun is coming up.

An exchange of *que pasos*, and then Costello asks, "You ever see an axolotl?"

Luis, eyes still bloodshot after his festival weekend in Zacatecas, shakes his head.

"It's a Mexican salamander," Costello explains.

"I saw a gila monster," says Luis.

"I've seen pictures of those things," says Costello. "Ugly suckers."

"The thing about them," says Luis, "is they don't have...they can't ever..."

"They can't ever what?"

"The tail just gets bigger," says Luis. "It fills up. Their whole life."

"What, with shit?" Costello readies a Tareyton. "Are you telling me gila monsters don't have assholes?"

"It just fills up."

"That's not healthful. Shit is toxic."

Costello considers a burrito. It will destroy him, but what the hell. He and Luis load up on chorizo and enter the pipe yard. Sunlight playing through a pyramid of bell-ended sixteen-inch PVC. The warehouse is twenty thousand square feet. Smells sweetly of diesel exhaust. Costello walks up the ramp that Jack installed for Linda and enters the dark and empty office. He passes through the catalogue library and into a wood-paneled war room. Jack is a giant eyebrow with a man attached. On his desk a double frame with pictures of his wife and kids.

Fluorescent light and the smell of a million burned coffees.

"Hold on," Jack says, and puts his hand over the mouthpiece. "Listen, comrade. I'm sending out an email. I'm outlawing consignments. Anything we ship from here we expect to be paid for. That's my new business philosophy. I'm speaking, what do you call it? Ex cathedra? You guys have too many funky arrangements going, and I'm too stupid to keep track. If you want, do sixty-day billing and address the receivable with Linda, but after that point we expect to be paid. That's what I'm going to say in the email."

"Gila monsters don't have assholes," Costello says, sitting down.

"Can I call you back?" Jack hangs up the phone. "Is that true?"

"The tail just gets bigger. The shit stores up in there and that's why they're poisonous."

"That makes sense from an evolution standpoint."

"Good thing humans don't work like that," Costello says. "That would be a major blow to our industry."

"Beautiful." Jack sips from his Styrofoam cup. "Listen. You need to talk to somebody at Bromberg. We need to get this ballcock thing taken care of once and for all."

"It's taken care of," Costello says. "That's all I've been doing. Lamrock was merciful. He signed off on everything."

"I'm still getting calls from everybody at Bromberg."

"One defective part and the whole universe unravels."

"I'm tired of the calls. I can't deal with those fucking people."

"I'm going out there on Thursday," Costello says. "I'll take care of it."

"Great," Jack says. "How's everything else?"

"Have you ever seen an axolotl? It's a white lizard with golden eyes."

"No, but there's a bat in Paraguay that can fly through the trees. It's got a powerful sonar. The sonar makes a hole in the tree and the thing flies right through."

"Things can't fly through other things," says Costello, "That's one of the laws of physics."

Jack shrugs, sips his coffee. This is the best part of the morning, bullshitting with Jack. Another lifer. Costello met him in 1972, when he was with Henderson Sales of Gardena, his first real gig. Started three weeks after his discharge. In the interview all they really wanted to know was if he played softball. They needed a shortstop. Destiny. Two years on the order desk, then inside sales, enjoying the air-conditioning. Then outside sales, flying around the country, a briefcase man, calling on big accounts in Kalamazoo, Adamsville, Port Arthur, and other cosmopolitan places. Phoning her every night from those ratty motel rooms. They once sent him to New York, his first and only time. He had visions of marble and light, a weekend full of banter, highballs, limousines, just like in the movies. But he was only there for twelve hours, taking a cab from JFK directly to a national distro center in Bedford-Stuyvesant. He did his presentation for all the managers and purchasing agents, and on the way out he met a valves rep coming through the door, Jack Isahakian, of the Glendale Isahakians, also on the East Coast for one day. An hour later, in the rain, they shared a cab back to JFK, neither of them so much as glimpsing the Manhattan skyline. It always turns out like that. Bummers and letdowns. Henderson eventually went under and Costello joined Summit Sales, which was basically just Henderson reconstituted without the baneful influence of Bob Henderson the price-fixing asshole who drove all of their customers away and died of a heart attack in the men's room of the Los Angeles Convention Center, thus securing his place in industry lore. Isahakian switched firms a couple times too. The years passing, they saw each other here and there, conventions, golf tournaments. Jack a diehard Dodgers fan. They always got along. Costello remembers telling him, at a counter day in Riverside in 1985, that he was putting in a pool. The last time Costello had money in the bank.

Then 1990, the plague. Summit went under. Costello was forty-five years old, hustling for a job, any job, making calls, pulling the girls out of Catholic school, sending them to the neighbors' for breakfast. Her minivan repossessed. Credit-card shell games. She started up an unlicensed daycare service, cash under the table, grocery money, a parade of little monsters splashing in the pool. She screamed at him at night, the kids awake across the hall. *You fucking bitch, I never took a day off in my life. Not one day.* But never out loud. Too scared of her. Just lay there, taking the blame. At one point he stopped by Home Depot and filled out an application to be a cashier. Worst day of his life. Then the call. Jack Isahakian, of the Glendale Isahakians, saying that he had nothing, absolutely nothing, because everyone was fucked at the moment, but, if Costello could stand to go back to where he'd started, he could work the order desk and maybe some days do outside stuff straight commission work on all the dogshit wholesalers, and see what happened after that, but everyone was fucked so no promises. Jack was a loudmouth, but a grinder, the real deal. What luck to know a good and honest man.

"Did you get the *Pipeline*?" Jack says, holding up his copy. "They cut half my quotes."

"It's still a nice little article."

"I heard from Lamrock's guy. WCPA is going all-out for the banquet this year. Prime rib, champagne, napkins."

"The decadence of Rome."

"When I win, they'll probably give me five minutes to make a speech. I'm using that gila-monster thing. It's beautiful."

Lights blaze in the outer office, marking the arrival of inside sales. Costello loads up on coffee and catalogues.

Going west on 91, against traffic. Costello, the driving virtuoso. Warehouses crowding both sides of the freeway. On each rooftop a row of spinning turbine vents. Silver spinning flowers. Costello sails over the bright and hostile neighborhoods of North Long Beach, scene of his wasted youth. The pool hall on Atlantic Avenue. During the plague, everything falling apart, he hid out there once again, a grown man, pretending he still had a job. Nine-ball at two in the afternoon. A vacation in hell. Smoke and mirrors for two months. Putting everything on the credit card. She said he looked gray, his skin was gray, and when he told her, finally, a moment of pure relief, she was there, touching his gray hand, bringing his color back.

Costello spends Monday night sitting in his chair, watching reruns of *Law & Order*. The phone rings. He never gets there in time, picks it up right when the machine turns on, creating stress and chaos for everyone involved. Gone for over a year and she's still the outgoing message. Talking over her voice, the machine beeping, the kids on the other end, annoyed.

"Dad?" one of the girls says. He can't tell their voices apart.

"Hello, hello!"

"It's Katie."

"Katie!"

"Watching the game?"

"It's a travel day. How's summer school?" She has to teach it for extra money. Teaching at a Catholic high school, a vow of poverty.

"I talked to Megan and Matt. We want to take you out on Saturday."

"Don't go to any trouble," says Costello. "You guys should enjoy your weekends."

"I'll call you Saturday."

"Okay. Well, I'll let you go."

"I don't need to be let go. I'm talking to you. We're talking."

"Okay."

"How's business?" she asks.

He tells her everything he knows about gila monsters and their lack of assholes.

"I don't think that's true," she says.

At lunch on Tuesday it's Costello vs. Luis. The warehouse crew gathering around the ping-pong table, eating pizza. Even after a few beers, Luis is nimble and cunning. A bottle of Advil rattles ceremoniously in his back pocket each time he lunges for a ball.

"Marty gets cute with the backspin," Jack warns, beer in hand. Next to him is Dave Mumbry, who took over all the dogshit accounts after Matt left.

"How'd you get so good at ping-pong?" he asks.

"The Army," Costello says. "It's the least selective fraternity in the world."

He hears someone calling his name. Lilac perfume mingling with diesel exhaust. He turns to where Linda used to be and then down to where she is. Linda, twenty-four years old with a bullet in her spine.

"Five Star Pipe and Supply," she says. "Is that your guy?"

"He was Matt's, but now he's mine again."

"They ordered some brass but didn't give me a PO number."

"Ron gave me a verbal," Costello says. "I gave them ninety-day billing."

"Ninety days!" Jack shouts. "What is that, philanthropy?"

Costello follows Linda up the ramp. Doesn't know whether to help push her.

"I'll put him on a payment schedule for that stuff," she says, "but nothing else leaves the warehouse until I see some money."

"I'll take care of it," Costello says.

Later that night, Costello pulls into his driveway. There's Rocha, revving up his Harley. And Connie running out the front door, encased in denim. Down to Chili's, for a delightful evening of pillage and rape. She waves to him and off they go, her legs squeezing tight.

The house is dark and quiet. For a couple of hours, Costello sits at the dining room table, paying the bills. Still paying off the bust. Fifteen years without a vacation. Never taking her out to dinner, not once. A million Ragú dinners. But at least they never ran out of rats.

Later he turns on the TV. The Dodgers on the first night of their home stand. Down two runs in the eighth. Costello, anxious, muttering to himself, drinking straight from the two-liter bottle of Pepsi. He wanders over to the glass slider and looks out on the darkness. He turns on the pool light. A pretty shade of green and the lizard down below.

• • •

Wednesday afternoon, up in Baldwin Park, a forsaken road winding past broken cinder block, a driveway with no address, a dungeon of a warehouse, and Ron Ciavacco, proprietor of Five Star Pipe and Supply. Sitting at the counter, marking up a racing form, as Valerie, his sister and only employee, smokes and watches *Dr. Phil* on a small black-and-white. They've been going out of business for twenty-five years.

"The wolf is at the door, my friend," Costello says, and gently explains the situation. The concept of paying for goods and services. Ron, a beggar and a chooser, asks for better pricing on globe valves. They shake hands. Ron wishes him luck at the WCPA awards banquet.

"I don't care about stats," Costello says. "Just as long as we win!"

At dusk, he hides from the eastbound traffic. Drives down Cherry Avenue, passing the cemetery on his way to the beach. The strand is dull and gray. Nobody goes in the water. He walks along the bluffs, smoking, counting the tankers in the harbor, a habit since childhood. Catalina Island, a distant mirage. Sixty years in SoCal and he's never taken the boat to Catalina.

Listening to the Dodgers game on the way home. Our man from Santo Domingo dealing a shutout into the seventh inning. Gets home just in time. Big bowl of vanilla ice cream, the last two innings, and then the news. Absolutely beautiful. There's a knock at the door.

"Hi, Marty!" Francine in her bike helmet.

"Now's not a good time."

She steps inside and Costello has no choice but to set her up with a bowl of vanilla. Be thankful for small mercies, Francine. The Nazis would have thrown you in a lime pit. Francine stares at the pictures on the bookcase, ignoring the travesty taking place right now in the top of the eighth. The manager, in his wisdom, pulling the young lefty after he gives up a walk. Let him work out of trouble, for chrissakes. Only way to become a pitcher.

"She said I could have her jewelry," Francine says.

"What?"

Francine walking down the hall, turning on the lights like she owns the place. There's no jewelry, no real jewelry, except her wedding ring. Katie has that. Francine in their bedroom, holding the rosewood jewelry box in her stubby hands.

"It's nothing fancy," Costello says. "You won't impress anyone, if that's what you're going for."

The box tucked under her arm.

"Fine. It's all yours. Come on."

Back down the hall, turning off the lights. Francine is going out the front door. She doesn't say goodbye. A Bedouin in the night.

The Dodgers closer gets lit up and they lose in extra innings. At eleven o'clock, Costello turns on the news. And then Megan calls, just to say hi.

He asks her about her junior college classes and she rants and raves about the stupidity of her fellow students. She hates Orange County. Fascist this, soulless that. She wants to travel. See the watery parts of the world. She talks through the weather and into the next commercial. Sports is next. Costello starts leaning toward the side table, getting ready to hang up the phone at his first opportunity. When he sees the Dodgers highlights coming on, he says, "Well, I'll let you go."

"What are you watching?" Megan asks.

"What? Nothing."

She laughs at him. "We're taking you out Saturday, whether you like it or not."

On Thursday afternoon he drives east into the Inland Empire, alighting upon a paved, semi-incorporated nowhere called Mira Loma. Bromberg Enterprises, the Death Star, sitting in a ring of smog on the edge of the freeway, five hundred thousand square feet of blazing white concrete. Costello parks at the edge of a vast parking lot and walks a half mile through warm, gusty winds that play havoc with his hair.

Through the dark maw of loading dock #53 and into the maze. Towering rows of everything. Hundreds of warehouse crew, pushing silver gleaming hand trucks and hydraulic jacks. It smells clean in here, no diesel exhaust, all the forklifts fancy and electric. A "No Smoking" sign every ten feet. At the far end a metal staircase leading to the offices of young men with advanced business degrees from accredited universities. It's only a matter of time before Bromberg swallows up Ajax and every other rep in SoCal. Death from above. Eliminate the middleman. Chris Easton, younger than Matt, but already with a wife and kids and a mortgage. A bureaucrat class and breeding, he sits Costello down, offers him coffee, soda, popcorn, hot dogs. They've got a whole circus up here. Costello breaks down the ballcock situation. Five hundred serial numbers for five hundred faulty units, written down by hand, his own, on a yellow legal pad, plus a flow chart of rebate and compensation. The factory rep running interference for the contractor, on behalf of the contractor's wholesaler, so neither have to face the wrath of the builder. The gallant factory rep, doing his duty, meeting his challenger. Pistols at dawn.

"It's ridiculous how complicated this is," says Easton, flipping the chart upside down.

"It's what they call a Byzantine arrangement. But I've already been out on all the job sites, squared things with Lamrock. We're switching out the defectives ourselves, all you need to do is sign off on the replacements so my contractor can pull from your shelves ASAP. The purchase order numbers are already plugged in and you get the percentage on everything. You really don't have to do a goddamn thing." Calm down, calm down. "I'm just saying…I'm just showing you what I did so I don't have to answer questions later. It's pretty much a done deal. Our long national nightmare is over."

"Lamrock okayed this."

"Ex cathedra."

"What?"

"Lamrock okayed it."

"Can you send this to me as an Excel sheet? I can't show this mess to my boss."

"You bet. There's a gal in our office. She's dynamite with computers."

Easton laughs, like he just heard a joke, and gives back the legal pad. A new bag of Pings in the corner, a framed photograph of Easton standing next to Tiger Woods.

"Are you going to the WCPA tourney?" Costello asks.

"Harbor Municipal," he says tentatively. "That's a pretty ghetto course."

"Not if you're a hack like me."

"They should have the tournament someplace nice."

"We're lucky there's still a golf course in Southern California that lets us play. Lamrock had to pull a lot of strings to make it happen."

"Have you actually met Lamrock?"

"If you have time," says Costello, "maybe we could go down and double-check your stock."

"It's all right here," Easton says, tapping his laptop screen. "Everything that comes in and out of here is all right here."

"I know. I just want to see it."

"Actually," says Easton, "I'm not allowed down there at the moment."

"Why not?"

"Long story."

"Oh, yeah?" Costello crosses his legs, getting comfortable. This is the job. This is the beauty of every job. Listening to stories.

"I don't have time to go into it. Just email me that sheet."

"Tell me the general area where I need to look. I'll use my Spidey sense."

"You'll get lost. I'll call somebody."

The liaison, a snaggletoothed black kid, arrives at the bottom of the stairs, driving an electric cart. Zipping down aisle 97B, a gob of tobacco under his lip.

"How come Easton stays up there?"

"Who?"

"Easton. He works upstairs."

The kid stops the cart and looks around. "A couple weeks ago, a dude got stabbed over by will call." Points ominously to a distant vector of the warehouse. "No one upstairs is allowed downstairs until the investigation is over. That side's run by Cucamonga Dogpatch. Northside Onterios are up here, running all the trim. Most of the foremen are Northside, so that's where the problem starts."

"Are you in a gang?"

"No."

"Well, Christ, be careful."

"The best part is that the guy who did it already got fired for something else."

"Does Easton know that?" Clever of young Easton, sending the old factory rep into the kill zone.

"No. We're all getting longer lunches while they do the investigation. Don't say nothing."

"I won't."

The kid gets him a mobile stair unit with suction stops. Costello spends an hour aloft, counting boxes one by one, then has a cigarette on the edge of the loading dock.

Later, driving back to Anaheim, against traffic, he pulls off to get some In-N-Out. Orders a double double animal style. Outside on the stone benches, a warm night, the sky gray and pink. Katie worked a couple summers here. Good money for fast food. Gave her acne. Or maybe it was Megan. Cute round face, both of them, like their mother. Would be nice if the kids could come to the WCPA banquet, be there when the awards are announced. But what a bummer for them, hanging around with a bunch of plumbers and toilet salesmen on a Friday night.

He stops at Home Depot and buys shock treatment for the pool. Waiting at the register. The girl trying to change the receipt, looking flustered. There but for the grace of God.

In the fading light Costello stands at the edge of the deep end. The lizard is barely visible at the bottom. He dumps in two bags' worth of calcium hypochlorite. Burns the nose. White cleansing death.

A year of radiation. A year of bedpans and vomit bowls.

Gray wispy hair like cobwebs on her head. *All so that we could have our long, precious goodbye. Pointless. It wasn't for you. I knew the young and dancing you. Disintegrating every day, pale, nauseated, dementia, that wasn't you. A thing died in our bed—it wasn't you. I should've slit your throat, babe, while you were still you.*

On Friday afternoon, before leaving the office for the tournament, Costello stops by Linda's desk and asks for help. He holds up the yellow legal pad containing all his ballcock calculations.

"Do you know how to put this in Excel?"

"Just put it there," she says, pointing to an empty spot on her desk.

"Doesn't have to be anything fancy."

She explains that she can email it to the guy at Bromberg as soon as it's done.

"Great!" Costello says. "Saves me the hassle!"

"You're late for the tournament," she says, shooing him away.

Harbor Municipal. Par-three wonderland. The parking lot full of plumbing trucks. One of them just a filthy old milk truck with no windows or decals. Instead, someone has traced "Kelly Plumbing" in the filth, along with a phone number. Blessed are the plumbers. Old guys in coveralls dragging their bags and beer coolers. Young vato plumbers in their Dickies, swinging wedges and putters.

Costello walks up to the ninth hole. Jack and Mumbry, totally blasted, are taking practice tee shots, trying to hit a foursome who are putting on the green.

"Fuck off," one of them yells back across the fairway, his voice muffled by the sound of the 405 freeway, which is hidden behind a line of eucalyptus trees.

Jack gives the guy the finger, takes a pull on his Tecate. Mumbry points to the sand trap by the green, where a solitary figure is sprawled facedown.

"That guy passed out down there about an hour ago."

"A hundred dollars if anybody tags him from here," says Jack.

"Maybe he's dead," Costello says.

"A couple guys from Dinoffria Plumbing reported back," Mumbry says. "He's breathing."

Ajax has a tent set up. Glorious standards flapping in the wind. A few plumbers stand around drinking, looking through catalogues, playing with the new faucet models.

Mumbry has orange chicken wing sauce all around his mouth.

"You missed the Hooter girls, Marty. They were giving out hot wings."

Jack puts an arm around Dave Mumbry. "Collectively the girls opted not to fuck Dave."

"I'm a married man," says Mumbry.

"So am I," says Jack. "It's a common condition."

Costello sits down on a folding chair. A young plumber is trying to figure out the action on the new ratchet cutters. Costello steadies a piece of one-inch copper and shows him how to clamp it on.

"Is this a sample one?" the plumber asks. "Can I have it?"

"What, free?" Costello shakes his head. "Not in this life, my friend. Who's your wholesaler? I'll have him bring some in for you."

What they call pulling business through. Costello gives the kid his card.

Sirens. An ambulance rolling up the cart path. Everyone scatters as it accelerates down the fairway.

"Maybe that guy is dead," says Mumbry, but the ambulance gets half-way to the green and makes a hard left, cutting through a tree line and onto another fairway.

"When's the best ball start?" Costello asks.

"It got canceled," says Mumbry. "There's some disorganization going on."

"Then fuck it. I'm having a whack."

Costello with a nine iron. Bend the knees, let it rip. Losing the ball in the white sky, then the silence of a distant landing, four feet in front of the sand trap. Costello grabs a wedge and putter.

"If I don't return," he says, "avenge me."

The grass is summer-brown. Hot winds whirling down from the freeway. Sirocco, an old crossword word. A ball whizzes past Costello's head.

"Incoming!" Jack's voice louder than the wind. Friendly fire. The drunk in the sand trap rolls over. Lying there, quite peaceful, with an empty bottle of peppermint schnapps next to his head, is the man himself, Lamrock, patron saint of plumbing contractors throughout the whole of Christendom.

Costello pitches his ball over the trap, over the corpus of Lamrock. The ball rolls onto the green. The flag, at first, is nowhere to be found. But then he sees it floating in the water hazard, along with several empty beer cans. Costello drops his putt, saving par.

A golf cart cresting the hill, plumbers dangling out the sides, wielding golf clubs and forty-ounce bottles of beer. A blond Hooters girl driving, swerving, laughing. She skids onto the green and someone yells, "Marty!"

Rocha, riding shotgun, has his arm over her shoulder. "Hey, neighbor! Are you loaded or what?"

"I'm just trying to get in a few whacks."

Rocha introduces his fellow technicians from Advanced Plumbing

Specialists, and his young cousin, an apprentice. He introduces Mandy.

"This is crazy," she tells Costello. "Most of the shit they send us to is so boring."

"Yeah, we have a lot of fun out here," says Costello, a little too brightly, voice cracking like a thirteen-year-old. Christ, the goofiness, it never goes away.

"Marty's nominated for sales rep of the year," Rocha says, drunk, grinning ear to ear, nudging Mandy with his shoulder.

"Wow!" Mandy says, with big mocking eyes.

Just once a piece like her, just once, but never. A bit trashy, but still, a time and place for everything.

"We're speed-golfing," says Rocha. "You have to hit the ball from the cart while it's moving. It's like polo."

"The sport of kings," says Costello.

"Which hole are we on?" asks the cousin, adjusting his ponytail.

"We're going backwards numerically, I think," says Rocha. "Hey, Marty, do you know Ron Ciavacco?"

"Sure."

"He had a heart attack on fourteen."

"Is he dead?"

"No, they put him in an ambulance."

"That's good."

A cart marked "Ranger" comes over the hill. A man armed with a bullhorn, yelling at everybody to go home. The WCPA Best Ball Extravaganza is drifting once more into chaos.

"Fascist motherfucker," says Rocha's little cousin.

Costello and Rocha extract Lamrock. His face plastered with drool and sand. They pour some water on him.

"It's prime rib time," says Rocha, nudging Mandy once more. "You like meat, right?"

A frozen smile. She looks trapped all of a sudden. Waiting for all of them to go away. They load Lamrock in the cart and drive up the fairway. Jack sees Lamrock and laughs.

"That was you down there? You fucking lightweight!"

"I think I got dehydrated," says Lamrock.

The Ajax standards coming down. In carts and on foot, plumbing contractors sweep across the steppes of the municipal course. The Mongol hordes. Costello helps carry the faucet displays back to the clubhouse, which is now off-limits. Through the windows the silver vats of prime rib.

The wait staff taking it all back to the kitchen. Security pushing plumbers from the door.

"Somebody tell somebody that Jack Isahakian wants to eat," says Jack.

A forty-ounce shatters on the pavement. Pushing and shoving. Security on their walkie-talkies, calling in an air strike, Lamrock trying to climb in through a window. Night falling on Harbor Municipal.

"I don't think they'll let us back next year," says Mumbry. In the end, the banquet gets held in the parking lot. The WCPA supreme council gathers everyone up and, just like that, the awards ceremony is over. Jack wins manager of the year. Mike Melendez, of Southwestern Sales, gets rep of the year. Costello congratulates Mike, who says, "That ballcock thing fucked you up."

Mike takes his trophy and leaves. Most of the guys head out, a cavalcade of plumbing trucks. Lamrock pouring shots into Dixie cups for everyone who sticks around. The lifers. The heavies. In the amber darkness, Jack mounts the hood of his Grand Marquis, holding up his plaque in triumph.

"Hey, listen up. I'm not leaving here without a speech. Somebody introduce me. No, fuck it. I'll do it myself. I'm Jack Isahakian. Some of you are lucky enough to know me." A chorus of fuck-yous. "Yeah, well, I'm a lucky man, myself. I work with a lot of highly competent professionals. Solid people, top to bottom. Warehouse, inside, outside. I can point to anyone at Ajax, man or woman, and say, 'That guy right there, he's a fucking pro.' Let me give you an example. I have five minutes, right? Most of you know Marty Costello. He's what we call a salesman. What he does is make sales calls. A couple months ago, on a rainy day, he walks in the door at Munson Pipe and Supply in Hawthorne." Some whooping and hollering from the Munson contingent. "That's what salesmen do. They show up and they walk through the door. On this day it turns out that our competition, who shall remain nameless….It's Gary Yeager from Carlton-Hill Sales. Is he here? I don't want to throw Gary under the bus or anything, but on this day he excused himself from walking in the door because it was raining outside. He actually called up Munson and said that. I admire his honesty, but if I felt I couldn't work because it was raining outside I wouldn't admit it to anybody. I'd go home and shoot myself. Anyway, our friends at Munson also thought it was funny, and since Marty the Brentford toilet rep was there instead of Gary the Kenner toilet rep, they thought, why not have Marty take a look at our inventory and see what's what? Forty items and ten categories later, Marty walks out of there with the biggest order of the year. And all he did was show up for work."

Jack drops his plaque. It hits the bumper on the way down and thuds on the pavement. "I had this thing planned about gila monsters, but it's getting late, comrades, and I've had a lot to drink."

A smattering of applause. Rocha and Mumbry laughing, shaking Costello's hand. The guys from Munson shaking his hand. Other wholesalers, plumbers, Lamrock.

"Somebody call Jack a cab," he says.

Saturday afternoon. The kids on their way. Costello has shocked them with an actual plan: dinner in Catalina.

But first a bit of sun. The pool turquoise. The glass slider sliding. The roof, the wall, the wires. This house is his. Or the bank's, but he still lives here.

Costello hops on the raft, pushes off, lights up. The telephone pole in the corner of the yard, like the mainmast of a ship.

He rolls off the raft and into the pure blue water. Down he goes to the bottom of the deep end. His eyes open, burning. The lizard pale from the chemicals. You never complained, not once, your hair falling out, the hideousness of your round beautiful face. That final moment, your green eyes popping open, and all the bile spilling out of you. A goddamn captain, going down with the ship.

Back on the raft, the lizard in his hand, pale and soggy, tiny black eyes and tiny white feet. Costello throws it over the wall and hears it splash in his neighbor's pool.

HELEN EVANS BROWN. Excerpt and "Avocado Salad" from *Helen Brown's West Coast Cookbook* by Helen Evans Brown, copyright © 1952 by Helen Evans Brown, copyright © 1991 by Philip Brown, Executor of the Estate of Helen Evans Brown. Illustrations copyright © 1991 by Sandra Bruce. Used by permission of Alfred A. Knopf, an imprint of the Knopf Doubleday Publishing Group, a division of Penguin Random House LLC. All rights reserved.

COLLEEN DUNN BATES. "My Father's Malibu." Copyright © 1997 Colleen Dunn Bates. First published in the August 1997 issue of *Westways* (Automobile Club of Southern California). Reprinted by permission of the author.

ERIC GUTIERREZ. "My Mother's Griffith Park." Copyright © 1997 Eric Gutierrez. First published in the November 1997 issue of *Westways* (Automobile Club of Southern California). Reprinted by permission of the author.

DANNY MARTINEZ. "Photo Essay: L.A. Ciudad." Photographs and essay copyright © 2018 Danny Martinez. Used by permission of the author. dannymartinezphotography.com.

WENDY GILMARTIN. "The Bank That Looks Like a Del Taco" and "The Zipper on a Pants Suit." Photographs and text copyright © 2012 Wendy Gilmartin. First published July 12, 2012, and September 4, 2012, respectively, in *LA Weekly*. Reprinted by permission of the author. www.wendygilmartin.com.

GINA B. NAHAI. Excerpt from *Moonlight on the Avenue of Faith* (Boston: Houghton Mifflin Harcourt, 1999). Copyright © 1999 Gina Barkhordar Nahai. Reprinted by permission of the author. ginabnahai.com.

ANN SUMMA. "Photo Essay: Urban Cyclists." Photographs and essay copyright © 2018 Ann Summa. Used by permission of the author. www.annsumma.com.

JIM GAVIN. "Costello" from the short story "Middle Men," included in the book *Middle Men* (New York: Simon and Schuster, 2013). Copyright © 2013 Jim Gavin.

SOURCES & ACKNOWLEDGMENTS (IN ORDER OF APPEARANCE)

Our contributors hail from many eras of L.A. literary life and write from many different vantage points. They're all in good company.

JOSÉ ARNAZ dictated some of his *Recuerdos* for the Bancroft Library in 1878. He was born in Spain in 1820 and studied medicine before heading to Cuba and to then-Mexican California. As a merchant, he first traded by ship up and down the coast before opening general merchandise stores in Los Angeles and San Buenaventura, where he settled. He describes the pueblo of Los Angeles in 1840 as being populated by "500 or 800 souls, nearly all native Californians."

COLLEEN DUNN BATES, a sixth-generation Californian, is publisher, founder, and editor of Prospect Park Books. She's worked as a writer and editor in radio, newspapers, magazines, and books. She is also the board vice president of PubWest, a board trustee of Immaculate Heart High School, and the L.A. restaurant critic for *Westways*. With Susan LaTempa, she is coauthor of the book *Storybook Travels: From Eloise's New York to Harry Potter's London, Visits to 30 of the Best-Loved Landmarks in Children's Literature*, as well as several editions of *The Unofficial Guide to California with Kids*.

RAY BRADBURY (1920–2012) was a prolific and influential American author credited by *The New York Times* with bringing science fiction into the mainstream through such books as *Fahrenheit 451* and *The Martian Chronicles*. He was awarded the Pulitzer Prize in 2004. Bradbury's family moved to Los Angeles when he was fourteen, and when still a teen he sold a joke to the *Burns and Allen Show*. He wrote more than thirty books, almost 600 short stories, and many screenplays, teleplays, and other works.

HELEN EVANS BROWN (1904–1964) was a noted author of cookbooks and was especially influential in the 1950s and '60s. With her husband, a rare-book dealer, she owned a collection of about 10,000 gastronomy books in French and English. She is best remembered for her *West Coast Cook Book* as well as for *The Complete Book of Outdoor Cooking*, which she coauthored with James Beard.

DIANA SERRA CARY is the author of several books, including *Hollywood's Children: The Inside Story of the Child Star Era*; *Hollywood Posse, The Story of a Gallant Band of Horsemen Who Made Movie History*; *What Ever Happened to Baby Peggy: The Autobiography of Hollywood's Pioneer Child Star* (the basis for the 2012 film doc *Baby Peggy: The Elephant in the Room*); *Jackie Coogan: The World's Boy King: A Biography of Hollywood's Legendary Child Star*; and others. She worked for many years as trade-book buyer for the University of California, San Diego. In October 2017, at 99, she self-published her first novel.

JIM GAVIN is the author of *Middle Men: Stories,* published in 2013. It is his debut short story collection. He was born in Long Beach, grew up in Orange, and attended Loyola Marymount in L.A. He worked after graduation at the *Orange County Register*. His fiction has appeared in *The New Yorker*, *The Paris Review*, *Zoetrope*, *Esquire*, *Slice*, *The Mississippi Review*, and *ZYZZYVA*.

WENDY GILMARTIN is a licensed architect and writer living and building in Los Angeles. A fourth-generation Angeleno, she is L.A. partner at FAR frohn&rojas, with offices in L.A., Berlin, and

Santiago, Chile. She is a visiting lecturer at California Polytechnic State University, Pomona and a member of the board of directors for the L.A. Forum for Architecture and Urban Design. She has contributed to the books *Latitudes: An Angeleno's Atlas* and *Best Practices*, and she was a columnist for *LA Weekly*. Her articles have appeared in publications including the *Los Angeles Times*, *Landscape Architecture Magazine*, *KCET's ARTBOUND*, and *The Architect's Newspaper*.

ERIC GUTIERREZ, writer and cultural correspondent, has been health policy director for the Los Angeles LGBT Center and prior to that was special advisor to the president for institute initiatives at California Institute of the Arts. He is the author of the book *Disciples of the Street: The Promise of a Hip Hop Church*.

CHESTER HIMES (1909–1984) was the author of nearly twenty novels, dozens of short stories, and two volumes of autobiography, among which some of the best known are *If He Hollers Let Him Go*, a now-classic account of wartime Los Angeles as experienced by a black protagonist, and *Cotton Comes to Harlem*, one of a series of mysteries set in Harlem but based on two L.A. policeman he knew, written after he had self-exiled to France, where he lived for many years.

NAOMI HIRAHARA is the Edgar Award–winning author of the Mas Arai and Officer Ellie Rush mysteries, both set in Los Angeles, and is a former reporter and editor for *The Rafu Shimpo*, L.A.'s English-Japanese bilingual newspaper. She is also the author of biographies, reference books, and a novel for young readers, *1000 Cranes*. *Terminal Island: Lost Communities of Los Angeles Harbor*, coauthored with Geraldine Knatz, received the Bruckman Award for Excellence in a Book about Los Angeles from the Los Angeles Public Library and the Award of Merit for Scholar/Authorship from the Conference of California Historical Societies.

CONTRIBUTORS

PRESTON LERNER is a Los Angeles writer whose work has been published in *The New York Times Magazine*, *Los Angeles Times Magazine*, *Sports Illustrated*, *Wired*, *Texas Monthly*, and *Travel & Leisure*. Formerly a contributing editor at *Popular Science* and a contributing writer at *Automobile Magazine*, he's now a contributing editor at *Road & Track*, often covering automobile racing. He's the author of one novel, *Fools on the Hill,*, and five books of nonfiction. His latest book is *Speed Read Ferrari*.

H.E. LOUGHEED's description of his father's innovations for harvesting wild mustard was published in January 1951, in *Westways*. He was a member of the Stanford University class of 1900 and later of the Lorquin Natural History Club in Pasadena.

BENJAMIN MADLEY is associate professor of history at UCLA. Madley is a historian of Native America, the United States, and colonialism in world history. He was born in Redding, California, and lives in L.A. His book *An American Genocide* received the *L.A. Times* Book

Prize for History, the Ralph Lemkin Book Award from the Institute for the Study of Genocide, the California Book Awards Gold Medal for Californiana, and other awards. The book was named a *New York Times Book Review Magazine* Editor's Choice, and at the 2016 Dee-ni' Night was designated an option for the Tolowa Dee-Ni' Nation's tribal gift, among other recognitions.

DANNY MARTINEZ is a freelance photographer from the Los Angeles area. His work encapsulates the gritty, the beautiful, the bizarre, and the artful that surround him at any given point. He first encountered photography on a deep level while taking a high school film photography course. He received his BA from California State University, Long Beach in 2007.

GINA B. NAHAI is a best-selling author, columnist, and emeritus professor of creative writing at USC. Her novels have been translated into eighteen languages, and she has received the Los Angeles Arts Council Award, the Persian Heritage Foundation's Award, the Simon Rockower Award, and the Phi Kappa Phi Award. Her writings have appeared in numerous national and international publications as well as in a number of literary and academic journals and anthologies. She is a monthly columnist for the *Jewish Journal of Greater Los Angeles* and is a three-time finalist for an L.A. Press Club award. Her most recent novel, *The Luminous Heart of Jonah S.*, was a finalist for the Jewish Book Council's fiction award in 2014 and long-listed for the Dublin International Literary Award.

NELLIE VAN DE GRIFT SANCHEZ (1856–1935) was a translator and romanticizer of the Californio period (*Spanish Arcadia,* 1929). She is best known for *The Life of Mrs. Robert Louis Stevenson*, a biography of her sister.

MICHELLE SHOCKED is a singer-songwriter. She lived on a houseboat in the Los Angeles harbor from 1989 to 1994.

ANN SUMMA has made award-winning portraits of the famous and not so famous for more than thirty years, has worked for many major publications, and has taught photography at Otis College of Art and Design for twenty years. Her photos documenting L.A.'s late-seventies punk subculture are collected in the book *The Beautiful and the Damned*. Her personal work explores underrepresented people of all ages and ethnicities working together to experience and create life as a radical departure from the stereotypes presented in mainstream media. She lives in L.A. and San Miguel de Allende, Mexico.

HARTMUT WALTER is a UCLA professor emeritus with research interests in biogeography, globalization impacts on nature, animal ecology, ornithology, and extinction geography. He leads bird photography walks for Samy's Photo School and is the author of *Eleonora's Falcon: Adaptations to Prey and Habitat in a Social Raptor*.

PHOTO BY DANNY MARTINEZ